The Chamber of Curiosity

Apartment Design and the New Elegance

gestalten

Content

Things as Ideas & Identity

By Shonquis Moreno

Our body is the first thing we own, which means that we are naturally and irrevocably bound to the material world and to things. But things represent opportunity as much as constraint: Belongings and how we live with them are our way of telling the world where we belong—or want to belong. They express our values and, if not what is true about us, at least what we wish to be true. If understood correctly, things, above all else, are ideas. This fact may explain the recent fascination with the medieval cabinet of curiosities, which moved into the popular consciousness and then into our living spaces. Casting off aesthetic uniformity and banal minimalism, interior designers are underscoring atmosphere and individuality through eclectic and painstakingly collected furnishings and objects. Using poetic contrasts, the eloquent naïveté of the artisanal object, unconventional juxtapositions, palettes, and bespoke materials, they are exploring the client's unique character, experiences, and point of view through space—with results that recall those marvels of long ago.

Ancestor to the modern museum, from the 15th to the 18th century, the cabinet of curiosities—or **Wunderkammer**—consisted of a room or series of rooms (**Kammer**) brimming with art (**Kunst**) and objects of wonder (**Wunder**). It was a place to store, study, and catalog the known and the unknown, a personal sanctuary and a showcase of both wealth and erudition. It was also considered a microcosm of the natural world, a space where awe, innovation, learning and mystery were privileged over tradition, conformity, and doctrine. This made it, not least, a baroque expression of its creator's unique view of the world.

That world was contained in an immersive interior over whose every surface were juxtaposed wildly eclectic objects: a crocodile mounted to the ceiling, seahorses, shrunken heads and once-living things dried, stuffed or bottled, human anatomy sculpted in colored wax, drawings of snowflakes observed through a microscope and the microscope, itself. "Rarities" included real fakes like Montezuma's feather headdress and outright inventions: the feathers of a phoenix, a mermaid's hand, fact and fiction living side-by-side, as equals.

Early on, every surface of the interior became a display, from the spaces between ceiling beams to every inch of wall, along with elaborately crafted, purpose-built cupboards and shelves, drawers and armoires and built-in cabinets whose faces unlocked to fold down. Taken together, these displays seemed serendipitous or arbitrary, but were neither. Instead, this **horror vacui** followed the intuition or logic of its designer: Objects were grouped to establish connections or reveal those that had been overlooked in order to see and think about the world in entirely new ways.

The power of the **Wunderkammer** lay in its relationship to the individual imagination. If the objects in the curiosity cabinet were actually exhibitions of their creator's intellect, tastes, memories or manifesto, so too are those in the contemporary interiors that, eschewing any particular style or trend, may be called "scenic": interior landscape, scenography or a little of both, they are driven by a personal point of view.

Collectors of Things

Often this means that the designer is their own client, or the client, their own designer and that each is, by nature, a collector—a collector reconstituting that early immersive microcosm of wonder. The scenic interior becomes the designer's cabinet, an experiential collage in which most objects, because they represent a point of view, are the character actors of interior design, precisely because they are built on character. The collector seeks objects everywhere, at all times: whether brand name or an anonymous piece of mysterious provenance (unicorn horn or narwhal's tusk?), they are not sought to suit a color scheme or contribute to a particular style. They are simply—and irrationally—loved, found now, and used when a use is found. Istanbul studio Autoban has found original pieces on the wheelbarrows of the Istanbul eskici, or junk sellers. Milan-based Dimore Studio found the weight plates for an old scale, but turned them into a pair of sconces. Designer Jean-Christophe Aumas returns again and again to the Paul Bert section of Paris' Porte de Clignancourt marché aux puces or when he travels, to a favorite flea market in Antwerp. These designers scavenge in junk shops on the way to auction houses and antique dealers. Beloved items are inherited from parents or knit by a daughter. Shinsuke Kawahara's Paris apartment is a warren of rabbits collected over years—porcelain rabbits, silver rabbits, a wooden rabbit carved in 1915—because they express his connection to Nature. Alketas Pazis is more than just a collector: He lives behind his Athens showroom in an apartment filled with industrial antiques with which he parts only reluctantly.

Relationships Among Things

In a sense, a cabinet of curiosities was like a koan. In order to fire the viewer's synapses in some fresh way, items entirely devoid of context (which is what happens to an object when collected) were grouped—poetically—around a theme of greater or lesser specificity. Similarly, the threads that connect objects in a scenic interior may be very subtle indeed. The designers edit and organize more or less irrationally, a peculiarly intuitive task that produces, among other things, a revelation of meaningful affinities and contrasts and a juxtaposition of unexpected objects into productive ecosystems.

But how to draw diverse objects together? One way is by throwing out hierarchy. Unlike minimalism, which can feel chilly and hollow or society homes—overwrought and impersonal—scenic interiors are surprisingly democratic, with junk store finds and limited editions on equal terms. Jean-Christophe Aumas pairs a daybed from Ebay with work by Gio Ponti, knowing that contrasts and unexpected connec-

tions reveal the most in the fewest "words." Aumas also clarifies this mashup by framing worthy things: colors frame fields of color, reflective surfaces frame the fine old wood of the floor, and hollow cubes frame emptiness, giving the viewer a delicious pause.

Through their editing and composition of interior still lifes, Milan-based Dimore Studio's combinations of objects seem too personal to be a style or decor. Their interiors are predicated on the fact that each complex object has been chosen for complex reasons, and integrated into complex scenarios with dissimilar objects—in a way that looks effortless. It is not single objects that make a space: "What really counts," says designer Emiliano Salci, "is the interaction each object has with those surrounding it." Dimore Studio's spaces are saturated with atmosphere because a compelling imbalance of extremes—thrilling and tranquil, obscure and familiar, humble and luxe—helps them manufacture mood. With light and shadow, they partition space into cubbyholes and niches, giving each vignette its stage without putting up walls. Scenic designers relate objects not just to each other, but to light, color, materials, forms, textiles, and texture.

For Italian designer Pietro Russo home is an expression of self: "The ambience must be a reflection of myself," , he says, "mirror my equilibrium and my contradictions. I see interior space as the scenery of everyday life." Color is a rich way to render these shifting aspects with immediacy: Dimore Studio borrow the chiaroscuro palette of an Old Master painting. Kelee Katillac consults her gem collection to mix paint colors. George Koukourakis exaggerates the jewel-tones native to his house on Nisyros, assigning vibrant hues to public space and tranquil tones to private quarters while, in a small Berlin apartment, Gisbert Pöppler blocks out fields of assertive color to lead the eye through space.

Fidelity to Certain Things

The scenic interior may express fidelity to time, place or person. To be true to an historical period or location, designers may bring in master craftsmen to restore antiques, match extinct colorways or replicate a window frame. David Hurlbut makes something new in the spirit of the old, using cheap plastic Halloween masks to cast classical sculptures. He also respects history by living with low-wattage light bulbs and large-scale furniture because the old electrical system can't support a bigger load and the building's stateliness would have swallowed anything smaller. Autoban reconcile elements from various time periods with contemporary pieces by layering them. Guided by the "aura" of a building, Pietro Russo designs many custom pieces: "Even in a home without furniture, anyone who enters feels this aura," he explains. "This aura is an expression of culture and should suggest the design direction."

Honoring time and place may also involve excavation — scraping the paint, peeling away layers of wallcoverings — and knowing when to stop. "If part of a building is beyond repair, work with what you have and leave the exposed area as-is," says Hurlbut who, on moving into his home, took a broom to the peeling original paint, but left what remained after a vigorous sweeping: a mosaic of uneven paint layers.

In the age of the cabinet of curiosities, conformity was a nearly universal value; today because the world has shrunk, it is an increasingly homogenous place in which individuality has its virtues. The rich details of a scenic interior are nothing if not true to its inhabitant: Dimore Studio designs very self-consciously to differentiate their clients. In the Carrer Avinyó holiday home shared by two brothers in Barcelona, David Kohn Architects designed a mosaic floor, featuring a triangular pattern that mimics the geometry of the architectural plan with gradations of color, from green at one end to red at the other, mapping out each man's domain. A dining table stands at the confluence of the red and green tiles, a graphical symbol of the gathering together of loved ones, of the home as a space of belonging — a microcosm of family.

Once, collectors saw the cabinet of curiosities as a microcosm of the natural world. And then we began to fathom and domesticate Nature. Today, it is our inner nature that is the mysterious macrocosm writ large in the scenic interior. We return "home" to find ourselves both marvelous and monstrous, rich and rare, fake and unfamiliar. Now we want to marvel at (and very occasionally, understand) our own natures, recover that gothic innocence — the flacons of perfume and dragon's blood lined up on the shelf next to the powdered mummies and poisons. No wonder: Without the curiosity, after all, it would just be a cabinet.

It is a cool, dark
world in which
some rooms
recall a theater or
cinema, promising
a cultivated,
creative, and
lush experience
punctuated with
brief thrills of
color.

Home of Artur Miranda and Jacques Bec

Oitoemponto design partners Artur Miranda and Jacques Bec designed their own home in Porto. It is a cool, dark world in which some rooms recall a theater or cinema, promising a cultivated, creative, and lush experience punctuated with brief thrills of color—petal pink, mint, purple, scarlet, gold—and the textures of steel, stone, and carpets with patterns carved into them. The rooms are populated with 20th-century modernist classic furnishings, a collection that includes a Joe Colombo Elda chair, a Harry Bertoia Diamond chair, an onyx-and-lucite coffee table in the style of Milo Baughman and Vladimir Kagan, sconces by Charlotte Perriand, and in the dining room a black Eero Saarinen Tulip Table surrounded by deep olive green Eames fiberglass armshell chairs on dowel bases. Neon signage hangs above a pair of canary yellow patent leather armchairs and a checkered tile floor, vignettes made up of pieces so full of character that they might almost speak to you.

Portugal // Oitoemponto

The Carrer Avinyó apartment in Barcelona's Gothic Quarter is a vacation home for two brothers raised in Barcelona.

The London-based architects underscored the building's rare triangular form to great effect. David Kohn Architects, who have done a one-room hotel for Living Architecture and exhibition design for the Design Museum, began with a bold gesture, tearing down the interior cross walls to transform the space into a single large corner room. They installed a mosaic floor with a triangular pattern that echoes the geometry of the plan and features gradations of color, from green at one end of the apartment to red at the other, that map out each brother's space. Shuttered birch plywood microarchitectural structures shaped like small buildings contain the bedrooms, mirroring the city outside by designing a small city within. The mezzanine library doubles as a series of balconies linking each room to its bath while, at the intersection of the red and green tiles, a DKA-designed dining table becomes a graphical symbol of the gathering of loved ones.

Spain // David Kohn Architects

Aside from its perch overlooking the sea, color, energy, and mid-century design classics from the 1950s through the 1970s define this 250 sqm residence in Monaco.

Monaco- and Paris-based architects Emil Humbert and Christophe Poyet preserved only one element of the original apartment: a salmon-beige marble floor, whose color and gloss they felt captures the glamour of its surroundings in consonance with the building's façade. As in much of their work, this chic dwelling celebrates purity of line and luxe, natural materials like stone, glass, and wood. Each room has strong protagonists: the office is screened by a wooden floor-to-ceiling shelf and cabinet unit and anchored by a heavy wooden desk with a single chevron-shaped leg. In the sitting room, the carpet has a stripey basketweave pattern and is paired with a stripey artwork and a pair of vintage French bentwood and rope armchairs by Audoux Minet.

Monaco // Humbert & Poyet

House P

House P

As he was designing Haus P in Berlin, Thomas Kröger reorganized the building in order to suit the modern lifestyle of a family of six people while still honoring and contextualizing the listed neo-classical villa, which was built in the 1930s. The architect imagined each space as a frame that contains, or even as a stage that presents, a mixture of legacy, vintage furniture, contemporary art and uncluttered spaces. He gave these diverse objects and materials generous space to breathe. The bathroom seems to have a breeze sighing through it, with its white walls papered with palm frond wallcoverings. In the library, Kröger constructed lacquered shelving from pine wood and bronze. Lacquered pine also features in the kitchen, along with travertine and a built-in leather sofa. Because Kröger designed—and worked with master carpenters to handcraft—built-in furniture and wall paneling, the new elements don't stand out conspicuously as new interventions. In fact, they appear to feel right at home with history.

Germany // Thomas Kröger Architekt

The Brussels home of a couple passionate about collecting 20th-century furniture is steeped in bright colors, contradictions, and a radical mix of styles.

To enliven the apartment and make it unique to themselves, the couple started by painting each room its own defining color. Actually it took many long discussions, but in the end they dressed the living room in English pea green, the office mallard blue, the kitchen pink, and the hallway Prussian blue. Addicted to searching for special pieces—the collection is nothing if not eclectic—they admit to re-arranging their apartment on a daily basis with new discoveries from auction houses, the web, or from dealers in Sweden, Denmark, Germany, and France and pieces by Charlotte Perriand, Ettore Sottsass, and Verner Panton. The rugs? Danish 1950s and a Moroccan kilim from the 1940s. In fact, the books that the two devour on their favorite subject have become an ornament in and of themselves, coloring walls of shelves across the apartment.

Belgium // anonymous

Home of Michael Minns

The walls of this East Yorkshire home are painted white, its wooden floors lacquered black. The interiors are canvasses for remarkable objects collected by the owner, including a few actual canvasses—large unselfconscious brushstrokes of color, perfect counterpoint to their containers. Designer and home-owner Michael Minns (owner of online design concept shop 47 Parkavenue), stripped the house down to "an unadorned blank canvas" before making each room home to a particular object or combination of objects. He pairs a vintage ceramic pineapple lamp with a table by Eero Aarnio, a pink sofa with a mid-century French bentwood and rope chair by Audoux Minet, a carpenter's work bench with a taxidermied zebra. The en-suite bath mash-up involves an Ikea rug, a stuffed kudu and a crystal chandelier hung from a garment rack at torchiere height. Minns' English eclecticism is effected with "wild abandon," he says. "I think it's a very English trait. We don't like things to be too perfect. There has to be an oddity or a strangeness amongst all the tradition."

UK // Michael Minns

Hansaviertel

Pöppler remade a 90 sqm apartment in a building originally designed by Walter Gropius that is a 90-year-old Bauhaus experiment in urban living, now owned by a celebrated local television writer. Pöppler broke up the boxy compartments that crowded and darkened the interiors partly by eliminating walls and partly through bold use of color blocking. The palette borrows hues used on the building's façade while, throughout, shiny black trim frames the color fields and serves as a unifying thread, tying each room to the next and eventually leading into the bathroom, where the threads fade into black tile walls. The designer married high and low-cost interior elements, including kitchen fixtures from Ikea that he dressed in Dedar textiles and combined with brass hardware. He also re-purposed and combined elements to compose a quirky kitchen: a GDR-era Sputnik chandelier and an antique farmhouse wardrobe that he turned into a cabinet, as well as a travertine display table and dressing-room doors that he found at the now-defunct German department store Sellbach. With two simple gestures, Pöppler mined the building for its own ideas, creating space, color, and light, and bringing it that much closer to Gropius' original intention: to create flexible city living.

Germany // Gisbert Pöppler

House on the South Coast of Spain

Victoria and Sylvia Melián Randolph's Spanish-American clients use this house on the southern coast of Spain year-round as a vacation home and, because they have several children, often entertain guests—adults and their many kids. For this reason, they asked the designers to create spaces that are casual, comfortable, and inviting. The architecture of the existing house was rational, so the design team responded with interiors that are simple, spacious, easy to maintain, and influenced by no particular historical period or style, only the needs of the moment. They organized the interiors so that all rooms open onto the garden, laid the floors with a local white stone, and opened up the structure to light as far as possible. In the sitting room, the team installed a cotton and wool rug woven to its design in Morocco. The sofas, sheathed in crisp white linen like the drapes, are also the studio's own design. In various shops and markets, they found a 1960s orange "Pastil" chair by Aarnio Arnio, sun mirrors, and the drum coffee tables. In the dining room, they used Bertoia chairs, old industrial lamps in orange that were also discovered in a flea market, a made-to-measure rug woven from esparto grass, and an ample dining table with industrial legs and a zinc top to welcome, of course, the greatest number of house guests.

Spain // Melián Randolph

Brooklyn Brownstone

Invited by a client with a love for pop art, vivid color, and modern design to remake their Fort Greene brownstone,

Helgerson's office took its inspiration from the patterns and colors common to Peruvian and Turkish rugs and textiles like the kaleidoscopic kilim installed in the master bedroom. In the dining room, the designers created a custom table comprising two long slabs of walnut connected by a series of butterfly joints and surrounded by vintage Paul McCobb chairs, lacquered in turquoise. Nearby, they painted a wall of bookshelves four shades of red and balanced these bright colors with the addition of herringbone oak floors and wood, ceramic and glass objects and furnishings. The globes of a David Weeks chandelier were then echoed by pendant lights installed in the kitchen. The family room is anchored by a built-in sectional sofa upholstered in 18 vintage Peruvian blankets, and a fir coffee table designed by JHID patterned after the blankets' designs. The artwork, three yarn-wrapped arrows, were made by Brooklyn artists. In the master bedroom and guest room, white and gray or violet and red paint slants up the ceiling and down the opposite wall, the pillows on the bed consist of remnants from the blankets used to dress the sofa, while mirrors reflect the geometric forms of terrariums suspended from the ceiling. From one room to another, the designers ensured that this Brooklyn couple will enjoy a colorful domestic life.

USA // Jessica Helgerson Interior Design

Brooklyn
Brownstone

Vacation Residence

This vacation home in southern Spain is a successful marriage
diverse objects and materials. The client was a family with childr
and dogs that also enjoyed entertaining frequently. The house w
built in 2002 but in subsequent years Victoria and Sylvia Meli
Randolph have grafted on pergolas, guest rooms, play room
saunas, and patios, allowing the house to grow with the family a
its evolving needs. The design team laid stone floors from Tarifa
the south of Spain in the kitchen, terracotta everywhere else, a
then whitewashed the walls. These white walls offset the designe
studied insertion of color throughout the house, as well as an ecle
tic and artful combination of objects. This anti-formula pairs artwo
from a Madrid gallery with a Moroccan carpet and a round wick
chair. In the kitchen, the designers created a custom pine table a
covered the sofa in a colorful botanic fabric by Swedish design
Josef Frank, accompanied by green Hans Wegner and Fren
Provençal chairs. Elsewhere, a round table and wicker armchair we
handmade in Malaga and wall tiles handcrafted in Lisbon, followi
a design conceived for the Lisbon Ritz Hotel during the 1950s. The
combinations and the strategic selection of both color scheme a
furnishings make the interiors entirely unique without freighting the
with preciousness or valuing things over peop

Spain // Melián Rando

Duplex in Madrid

Local designers Victoria and Sylvia Melián Randolph designed
this duplex in Madrid for a Mexican artist with strong tastes and
a passion for color, who was willing to let them take some risks.
Because the architecture of the apartment was poorly defined,
they could be as eclectic in creating a new identity for the space
as they wished and take advantage of a number of special existing
features like high ceilings with no moldings and wooden floors. The
designers' use of robust monolithic fields of color was supplemented
with multichromatic spaces like the patio, which are shot through
with a single color that dominates. In the bedroom, they combined a
tufted white linen headboard with raucous yellow walls and furniture.
The designers found a triptych mirror in the Rastro flea market along
with some wire shelves while the photograph of Picasso was bought
at auction. The studio finds many of the design elements it uses in
specialty shops and flea markets—not specified, but discovered
because they are unique. The result is a series of rooms rife with
color and unusual artifacts that synthesize many styles and periods.

Spain // Melián Randolph

Spot: A Fictional Interior

Nina Yashar, founder of Milan's Nilufar Gallery, approaches interior design as a form of exhibition that combines design, art, and architecture in various measures. Spot exemplifies this interdisciplinary, eclectic, and theatrical approach in the form of a fictional domestic space that challenges the viewer to question the value and status of the items in the room. Yashar wants visitors to Spot to think of design and art in discrete terms. The concept behind Spot's look and feel is a conflation of cultural, geographical, and architectural spaces with the notion of "nomadism," a quality that the designer identifies with personally. What Yashar is trying to communicate to her audience is that every object both has a history or story, and has the capacity to tell that story. This can be the story of who designed it, crafted or produced it, where it has been, how it has been used, and by whom. These stories elevate the object, as Yashar has said, "from contemplative to active," enabling it "to converse with its surroundings."

France // Nina Yashar, Nilufar

Loft in Turin

In a former factory in an old industrial area of Turin, the interior of this luminous home is mapped into three zones for socializing, eating, and fitness, and the design is guided by contrasts: inside and out, hard and soft, light and dark. Natural confronts artificial in the form of parquet wood flooring with the organic look of worn leather which is juxtaposed with inorganic resin floors. The hall leading to the bedrooms has lacquered-looking scarlet walls, a lavender floor, purple door, and an irregular ceiling hung with salvaged industrial neon banner groups. The past contrasts with the present through the preservation of what the designers call "the building's memory," the use of existing structural columns and original concrete industrial ceiling beams. This is paired with the insertion of new glass walls that make the most of the abundance of daylight and, scattered through each, islands of vintage furniture and contemporary art objects that promote a sense of discovery as one moves through the interior.

Italy // MG2 Architetture

Loft in Turin

Home of
Jean-Christophe Aumas

In creative agency artistic director Jean-Christophe Aumas' apartment frames proliferate: yellow line frames pink wall, frames are layered upon frames, some frames frame canvasses, other frames frame nothing at all. A mirrored credenza frames the canted reflection of Aumas' driftwood-like herringbone parquet floor. The high ceilings frame fields of vivid color—lemon, cobalt, rose, black. Even the boxy white dining room pendant lamps, outlined in black, frame themselves. Moving in, Aumas turned a guest room into the kitchen, and turned a hallway into a walk-in closet. Aumas designs store windows and events for brands like Céline, John Galliano, and Lacoste (for Printemps, he once used real sheep and birds in a display). This means he made many objects in the apartment; others he finds in specialty shops, flea markets, or on Ebay and there is no hierarchy of objects, high and low. Aumas sees the apartment as a laboratory in which any new object might be a catalyst for change.

France // Jean-Christophe Aumas, Voici-Voila

Jean-Christophe Aumas

Visual Art Director, Voici-Voilà // Paris, France

Framing Memory

say something, that represent a part of your personality, a place that tells little stories and creates images of your life."

Aumas' home is an apartment in Paris' 10th arrondissement. When he moved in, Aumas did most of the renovation work himself, turning a guest room into the kitchen and a hallway into a walk-in closet, and opening the space up, with glass walls or walls torn down, to bring in more light.

Today, the apartment's contents are not explicitly "organized," there is nothing fastidious and overthought, but the space contains, or frames, frames of many sorts, a tool Aumas uses in myriad forms in his window display design projects. Some frames frame artwork and photography, of course, but they also frame subjects that would ordinarily be treated as periph-eral. Aumas designed a gold-mirrored credenza that frames the reflection of his worn-as-driftwood parquet floor. An entirely black wall enigmatically frames three small blue triangles in its upper right corner, as if it is a page that could be turned with one's hands. The high ceilings and walls frame emphatic fields of color like this—black, lemon, midnight blue. He has painted half of one wall powder puff pink and then underlined it in yellow. In the dining room, each boxy lobe of the suspended white ceiling light is outlined in black, framing itself. In the bedroom, he has outlined another angular pendant light but drawn the lines of black outward to radiate over the ceiling, framing it too. Created for a Sol LeWitt-themed Louis Vuitton event, painted wooden cubes, rather the outlines of cubes, frame nothing but air. What is most

At its best, the design of a "home" is in service, not just to storytelling and emotion, but to a particularly gratifying form of self-expression. It is a space for the constant sloughing, morphing, and claiming of identity. For the visual art director of creative agency Voici-Voilà, Jean-Christophe Aumas, "home is a space with lots of memories—a mix of objects, pictures, and furnishings that

> "Home is a space with lots of memories— a mix of objects, pictures, and furnishings that say something, that represent a part of your personality, a place that tells little stories and creates images of your life."

clockwise:

1 Jean-Christophe Aumas, creative director of Voici-Voilà creative agency

2 Aumas uses frames to define space, from framed artwork to the gold credenza he designed that frames a reflection of the original parquet floor.

3 Beside an Arne Jacobsen Swan sofa, Aumas hung a photo of a mid-century chair.

interesting about this oft-repeated design element is that by using frames and fields of color, instead of giving the space structure, Aumas is actually deconstructing it, refusing to commit to the simple, limiting box of a room.

Aumas earned his degree in arts and textiles in 1991 after taking his baccalaureat in arts and literature three years earlier. He went on to become responsible for Louis Vuitton's windows and visual merchandising and then Cacharel's visual identity. In 2006, he went solo, establishing Voici-Voilà in order to specialize in visual art direction—windows and merchandising, sets, special events,

packaging, and catalogs—for international taste-makers like Lacoste, John Galliano, Chloé, Diptyque, Tsumori Chisato, Hermès, and Marni. For Paris department store Le Printemps, he once famously used real sheep and birds in a display window.

This experience means that Aumas has made many of the objects in his apartment (including the photography). He thinks of his home as a laboratory in which any new object might become a catalyst for change. It is a field for

experimentation and play for their own sake, not for the sake of testing design concepts that will later be applied to commissions for clients. Aumas separates the design of his domestic life from his professional life even if his sensibility and approach are shared by both. He can't identify a particular composition, material or object that dominates his work, but his particular combination of objects is distinct and the gleefully ephemeral nature of his design—whether it is his house, precipitously reinvented based

Aumas has an innate talent for forging relationships amongst diverse objects that would otherwise seem to have nothing in common: items found at auction houses, antique dealers, in design shops and flea markets.

on the purchase of a new sofa, or a vitrine that won't exist for more than a few weeks — makes it all the more intriguing. Nothing is ever fixed in place, change is imminent at all times.

Though Aumas' design solutions ultimately spring from the space itself, he looks for and serendipitously finds objects all over the world during his frequent travels. Antwerp is a favorite place to look for buried treasure and in Paris he frequents the sublime Paul Bert section of the Porte de Clignancourt flea market. The discoveries made in these places serve as both raw materials and tools that allow him to transform his ideas and moodboards into real space.

Aumas has an innate talent for forging relationships among diverse objects that would otherwise seem to have nothing in common: items found at auction houses, antique dealers, in design shops and flea markets. He makes them look not just beautiful together but engaging instead of merely random. He does this intuitively, however, not according to any formula: "I think it's completely instinctive the way that I mix objects. I have done many merchandising projects for my clients, so I'm used to mixing things together according to my own logic," he explains. "I like to mix

clockwise:
1 Aumas opened the space up to more light, but retained original elements like the chevron parquet floor.
2 Aumas uses color unconventionally, including painting the ends of firewood logs.
3 Color is used in fields throughout the apartment and rarely covers an entire wall.

"I like to mix and match things, old and new, and how I tell a little story really depends on my mood."

and match things, old and new, and how I tell a little story really depends on my mood."

The seemingly casual display of well-loved objects in the designer's house is a product of his belief that no hierarchy exists, nor should it exist, among objects. He introduces a scene or an entire scenography through invariably democratic, deftly manipulated compositions: a daybed from Ebay reupholstered with fabric from

Kvadrat co-exists with pieces by David Hicks, Gio Ponti, Warren Platner; Tom Dixon's Slab coffee table with Charlotte Perriand stools; an Arne Jacobsen Swan sofa that has been set beside a single panel of wallpaper depicting the photograph of a mid-century molded wood chair and nearby, a stuffed deer, a disco ball. Aumas knows that it is precisely the contrasts and the unexpected relationships that say the most to us, in the fewest words.

Apartment in Mayfair

Designer Francis Sultana's Mayfair apartment is signed a thousand times by the designers and artists whose unique objects and objets populate it. But while these uniquely authored objects are engaged in an engrossing "conversation" among themselves, the authorship of the interior, as a whole, is all Sultana's. His detailed and sure-footed combinations revel in a scaled-down grandeur and thrive on contrasts. In fact, the space serves as a gallery of the designer's widely ranging tastes. Sultana doesn't try to reconcile opposites; instead he lets them gossip, sing, chat, and hum. An emerald green upholstered chair by society decorator Emilio Terry and gray velvet, sequin-cushioned sofas designed by Sultana coexist vociferously with an aluminum console and silver Ring table by Mattia Bonetti, Fredrikson Stallard's King Bonk chairs, and shelves custom-designed by Zaha Hadid. Sultana's pop dissonance is colorful, dynamic, and extroverted: Versailles meets Warhol. A large space for entertaining connects, through grand double doors, the dining room to the high-ceilinged, parquet-floored living room. Nearby, in a wardrobe-sized former cloakroom, he has installed an original Victorian Thunderbox lavatory. His art ranges from Dinos Chapman sculptures, Paul McCarthy paintings, and Richard Prince prints to early Wolfgang Tillmans photographs and Grayson Perry ceramics. Their difference is the common thread amongst these objects. In Sultana's hands, this makes them a family of big personalities that live between white walls that are as neutral as they are joyfully cacophonous.

UK // Francis Sultana

Sultana's pop dissonance is colorful, dynamic, and extroverted: Versailles meets Warhol.

Library House

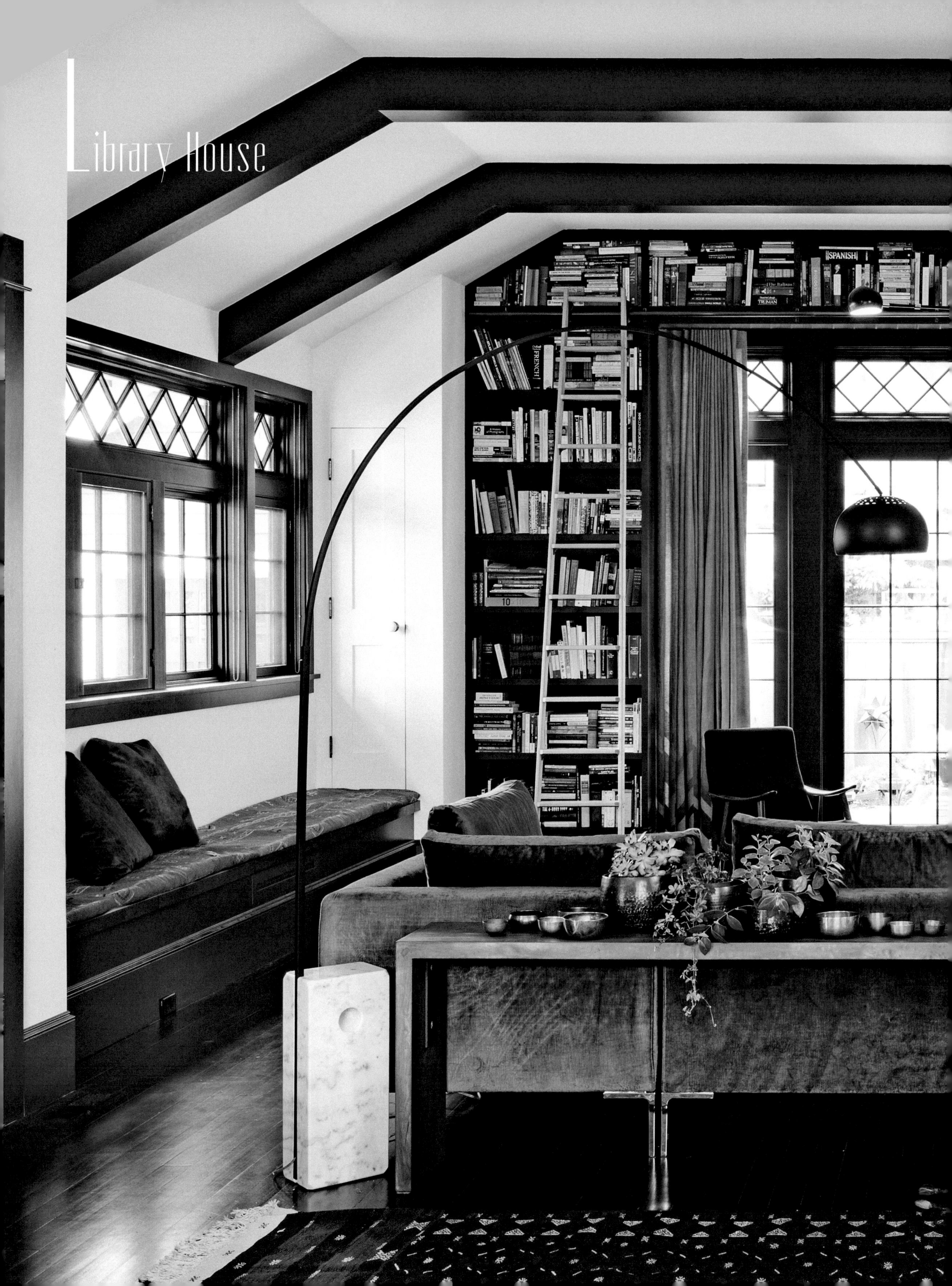

Library House

This residential design by Jessica Helgerson involved the reinvention of a Portland public library building that had also served, temporarily, as a church meeting hall. Helgerson's design team kept the large open volume of the former library, locating a kitchen, living room, and dining room there. By closing off the front porch, they shaped a foyer and powder room and by extending one flank of the building were able to add two bedrooms and a bathroom. In the basement, they inserted a sauna, laundry room, gym, and recording studio (both clients are voice actors). The plan is defined by bookshelves through-out the house—at the entrance, on both sides of the library's great room, in the guest bedroom—that honor the history of the building. To reach those in the high-ceilinged great room, library ladders were set at both ends of the room. Although many components of the interior scheme are traditional, like the original architecture, the designers layered contemporary elements over them.

USA // Jessica Helgerson Interior Design

The plan is defined by bookshelves throughout the house that honor the history of the building.

Home of Alketas Pazis

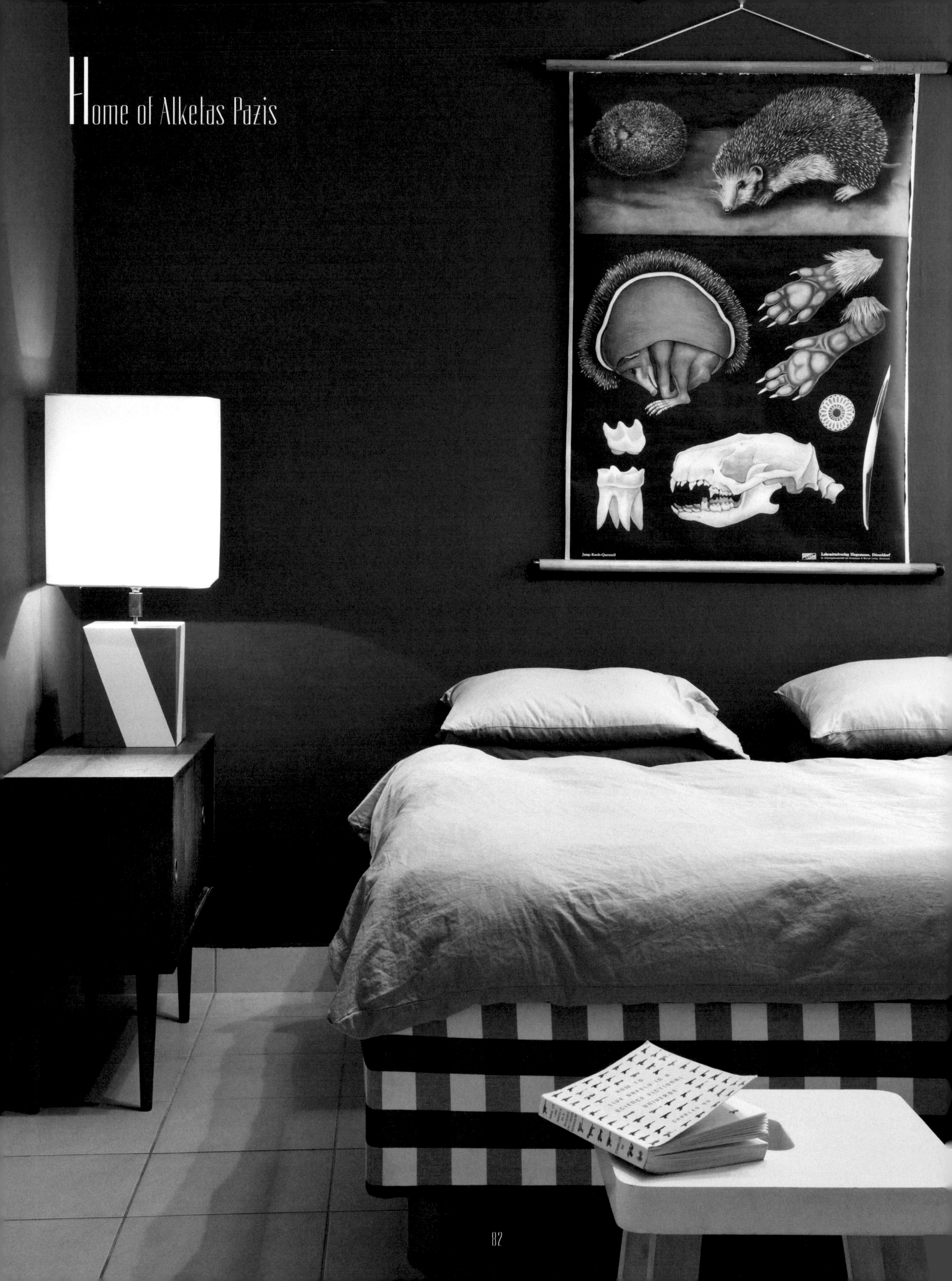

In designer and collector, Alketas Pazis' Athens home eclectic modernism dovetails with industrial antiques and inside he lives out his passion for early to mid-20th century objects.

Pazis lives behind the Temporary Showroom, a trading house for pieces from his collection, with myriad storied artifacts: a tall, many-drawered apothecary cabinet, fencing swords and masks, sailing ship models and globes, task lamps and natural history illustrations. The house retains its original mosaic tiled floors to which Pazis added family heirlooms, including carved cabinetry and Persian rugs. Wall lights hang from the ceiling and the tufted leather sofa recalls an Edwardian gentleman's club. Found in old public buildings like hospitals, schools, gymnasiums, and factories and sold at auction or discovered in flea markets, the objects that adorn Pazis' home lend the interiors an aura of days bygone while also, because of their eclecticism, feeling timelessly modern—many discrete histories coming together momentarily to tell one man's story.

Greece // Alketas Pazis

Spare & Dynamic in St. Kilda

In the studio's St. Kilda residence, Phelan balances spare but warm zones with dynamically eclectic areas. For example, the kitchen is wrapped in mid-century modern fields of grainy wood paneling set flush in the walls along with a large marble island, crisp of line, collared with red lacquered bar stools. By contrast, this elegant simplicity is alternated with a space like the crowded fireplace mantel or the dining room, which is aflutter with things: a tall bookshelf, a mylar pendant lamp by Marcel Wanders for Moooi. In interstitial spaces like the corridor and staircase, both aspects meet: the hall is a river of colorful Eastern floor tiles banked with white Western wall moldings while the wall flanking the stair is painted with a huge, nearly calligraphic stroke of red and green paint. As they found it, the existing Victorian structure proved to contain a rambling series of large but disconnected spaces, which had been installed during a flawed 1960s conversion of the building into a collection of discrete apartments. Phelan's team eliminated the 1960s interior additions to excavate the original rooms, which they reorganized to generate more light and a more organic circulation between interiors. Where the old structure was more complex, the new one has been rationalized and simplified to create a modern single family home that is both highly functional and eminently user-friendly.

Australia // Kerry Phelan Design Office

In the studio's
St. Kilda residence,
Phelan balances
spare but warm zones
with dynamically
eclectic areas.

Bofill has alternated between utopian social projects and neoclassical, rational monuments that privilege grandeur and symbolism over the human scale.

La Fabrica:
Ricardo Bofill Residence

In 1973 Spanish architect Ricardo Bofill adapted a disused, century-old cement factory outside Barcelona: 30 silos, subterranean galleries, and machine rooms made up of heroic concrete volumes. Amidst the Dali-esque ruins of this temple to industry were stairs climbing to nowhere, orphaned walls, buttresses abutting air, and reinforced concrete structures supporting nothing at all. Bofill's reinvention took two years, demolishing strategically, and turning eight silos into his home and the Taller de Arquitectura offices. Inside, interior designer Marta Vilallonga used as few new materials as possible to retain the power of the original architecture while making the spaces eminently livable inside. >>

>> Vilallonga exposed original wooden beams, coated cement, and brick walls with a blush of iron oxide paint, punched windows through them and draped them with monumental white curtains fit for Olympus, itself. Bright blank-white floors and furnishings were augmented with potted plants and wooden seating sculpted by Catalan artisans. Bofill has alternated between utopian social projects and neoclassical, rational monuments that privilege grandeur and symbolism over the human scale. With Vilallonga's help, La Fabrica synthesizes both, relocating the source of inspiration, ingenuity, and reverence not outside the human being, but within.

Spain // Ricardo Bofill, Taller de Arquitectura

La Fabrica: Ricardo Bofill Residence

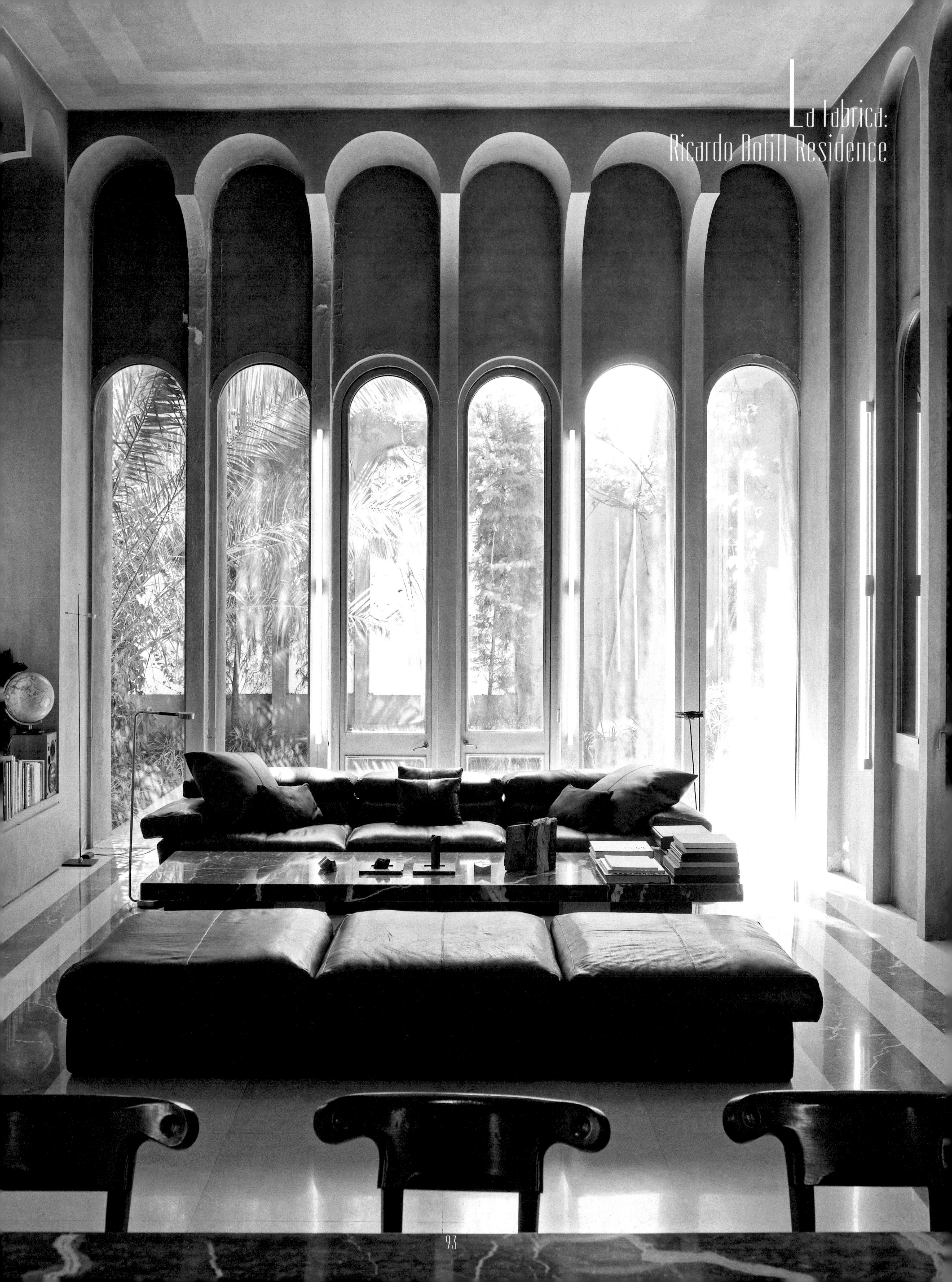

Timeless Space in Melbourne

Collaborative Melbourne studio Kerry Phelan created this Regency-style residence during a three-year restoration and addition that left it with an aura of bright natural white, gray, and silver that amplifies the presence of the colorful objects it contains. In fact, it took a great deal of time choosing, for example, the "Timeless" shade of gray paint by Dulux that would best accompany the client's artwork. Bespoke furniture designs by KPDO and details like globe lights from Roll & Hill, and classics such as tables and purple velvet chairs by Eero Saarinen or Busnelli are supplemented with unusual pieces that bring warmth to the bare contemporaneity like a vintage kilim, vintage Danish vases, a mirrored sideboard by Ilse Crawford, and copper and silver coffee tables from e15. White powder-coated steel doors open the dining room to the kitchen, which is also white, including gray-veined white Calacatta marble surfaces that introduce an organic pattern within the blank page of the space and are warmed by a gray oak timber floor. At the top of a black and white spiral staircase, bedrooms are floored with wide wooden planks and lush carpets. As Phelan interiors often do, the residence relies on few, strong details set within a fine neutral frame to become picture perfect.

Australia // Kerry Phelan Design Office

Timeless Space in Melbourne

Embracing Place

Talk about an interior that is "scenic," as in designed to embrace its place: For a Parisian couple in love with the area, architects Guy and Aurelien Allemand found inspiration for their renovation of this pine-shaded holiday home in the oyster fishermens' and tchanquée huts common to the Bay of Arachon. The architects combined interior and exterior by cladding the façades and inside walls of the 90 sqm house with Douglas pine, painting them in a serene gray, taupe, cream and chalk palette and using the same suspended industrial light fittings both inside and out. The library is furnished with a pendant fireplace, mid-century Scandinavian armchairs and a triple-branch lamp found at the Serpette flea market. Upstairs, they opened the bedroom up to a view of the water and, again, paired taupe and chalk in its color scheme, giving it a feeling of tranquility even while the cathedral roof lends it grandeur. From the podium bed, purpose-built by local carpenters, they framed the bay, bringing it indoors.

France // Guy and Aurelien Allemand

Mid-century Mashup

In the center of Tours near the chateaus of France's Loire Valley, this residential interior mixes craft with industrial design, and era with era.

For 20 years, interior designer Philippe Thelin has handled the structural aspects of each project while partner Thierry Gonzal creates the décor, but both are collectors at heart. Their deep knowledge of vintage design informs their work and fills their spaces with allusions to different time periods and aesthetic movements. They bring together a desk by Pierre Paulin and a Knoll armchair by the Eames with bronze and ceramic objects made by Yanneck Tomada and ceramics by Jules Agard. Canvases by Béatrice Devaux, Marie Duclos, and Picasso live with a Shogun Lamp by Mario Botta, composed neatly on the fireplace mantel, and a lamp by Sarfati. Most pieces have their provenance in the early mid-century period between the 1930s and the 1960s and are interwoven with a complexity that makes the house simple down to the smallest detail.

France // Philippe Thelin and Thierry Gonzal

Rue de l'Université Apartment

Jean-Louis Deniot's interiors synthesize the eclectic with the symmetrical, balanced, and legible, the eclectic with both luxury and serenity. His interiors, like the Louis XIV and Neo-Roman style apartment on Rue de l'Université, allude to various eras and movements without featuring them wholesale. They are "emblematic" interiors, full of archetypical furniture, ranging from Neoclassical through the 1930s, 40s, 50s, 60s, conflations composed with a sure hand. They represent the confluence of diverse personal influences, as well, from Adolf Loos' precision to Dorothy Draper's scenography. He establishes common ground among this polyphony of styles by drawing them into architectural vignettes, and by favoring (and designing) luxe objects and noble materials—mother-of-pearl, mica, malachite, bronze and parchment, opaline and shagreen. These provide the highlights of an otherwise subdued palette. Deniot appreciates many shades of gray. For him, luxury is not just a living idea, but an idea that lives through things.

France // Jean-Louis Deniot

Casa di Ringhiera in Milan

This 90 sqm home in the center of Milan was designed by Italian architect Paolo Rizzo in a casa di ringhiera, a vertical multifamily structure built between the 18th and 19th centuries. Rizzo cleared sightlines to form an airy, bright white box with lossy resin floors, soaked in natural light from skylights and sliding glass doors onto a terrace. Situated under the A-line roof, the ceiling assumes a cozy slant. Because Rizzo is a collector at heart, the object of his first passion now lives in the apartment: an Arco lamp by the Castiglioni brothers that once graced his parents' home in Sicily. Other design classics that furnish the space are a replica of Mies van der Rohe's 1968 Barcelona daybed, a Slab Chair by Tom Dixon, a Corallo chair by the Campana brothers. It is an interior design that allows its inhabitants to live, not just with light, but with inspiration.

Italy // Paolo Rizzo

Lorenz Bäumer Apartment

Louis Vuitton jewelry creative director Lorenz Bäumer is married to hospitality maven Géraldine de Fouquières with whom he designed their Parisian apartment. Bäumer, who wants to demonstrate the vivacity of French jewelry arts, accomplishes precisely this through interior design. It is a place of unabashed experimentation, accessorized ecstatically with rare objects and pieces that really stand out. With such pieces, it is difficult to create harmony because every single one has so much character, but harmony is not what the couple is trying to achieve. Pieces include, for instance, collages by Vik Muniz, chairs by the Campana brothers, lights by Ingo Maurer, metal sculptures by Yonel Lebovici, and a carpet by Hélène de Saint-Lager. The apartment has been described by bloggers as "anti-minimalist chic." But it could more simply be compared to a jewelry box. In this place, from whence minimalism has been exiled, Bäumer has invoked his jewelry muse on an architectural scale.

France // Bäumer & de Fouquières

DAKU 0006

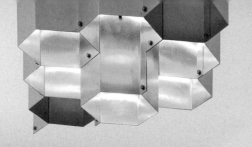

50 sqm in Città Studi

Pietro Russo's apartment confronts the modern-day dilemma of limited living space, but was shaped by not just constraints, but by possibilities. In the 50 sqm space, he kept sightlines clear while maximizing storage by creating custom furnishings that read horizontally or by occupying walls to their full height. He creates details himself from scratch or using discarded pieces (like tennis racquet fruit bowl shelves), his mantra being "adjust and adapt." In the kitchen, he allowed the confusion of partly removed layers of soft pink and orange paint to form a serendipitous tapestry that he then outlined in the shape of a life-size elephant. The illustration warms the severe concrete block of the kitchen counter, a "workbench for food." Russo adds personal details liberally. "The walls I see as a skin that protects the organs or that could become a container of meanings, so in every corner of the house I have messages for the future hidden in the walls."

Italy // Pietro Russo

House of Adriano and
Silvia in Milan

House of Adriano and Silvia in Milan

Milanese designer Pietro Russo earned a degree in scenography, and his interiors are nothing if not scenic. This interior bows to the 1930s building it's in, but only as Russo's ever-idiosyncratic interpretation of the period would have it. Inspired by the architects of old who designed comprehensive environments from architecture to furniture and chair to drawer handles, the designer generated visual continuity while injecting his own bespoke additions, including a strutted book-shelf and a minimalist tube light hanging from the molded ceiling of the living room. Russo retained the existing stucco, moldings, wood paneling, and a bow window, to reboot the original "aura" of the space, lost during poorly executed 1970s renovations. Russo made the bedroom more intimate by placing a large parasol-like ceiling light by Constance Guisset overhead and painting one wall sky blue. The bathroom—where floors, washbasin, and shower tray were made entirely from a single block of black Marquina marble—is also an allusion to the glamour of the era.

Italy // Pietro Russo

Pietro Russo

Product, Furniture, & Interior Designer, Artist & Scenographer // Milan, Italy

The Scenery of Everyday Life

50 sqm and two rooms. Because Pietro Russo's Milan apartment is small, the designer conflated living room and bedroom, using a single caned folding screen to mark the divide. The rich spareness of the objects and finishes in the room, as a whole, however, stand in stark contrast to the modesty, even asceticism, of his bed—which is all the bed "room" contains—as if Russo's dream life consumes all his waking hours and sleeping is merely something his body must do.

Russo's interiors are a map of the person who lives there. They are influenced by personalities and histories, and by constraints as much as opportunities. They rely on the handmaking of bespoke pieces and the establishment of relationships among diverse objects that will live together. He also makes a virtue of whatever materials and tools he has at hand—not simply to be resourceful, but because they represent the history of the space or the story of his client. Russo fashions atmospheric space, well-crafted, sophisticated, and eloquently naive. His own home, in a late 1930s modernist building in east Milan, exemplifies this: "The ambience must be a reflection of myself, mirror my equilibrium and my contradictions," he says, as he would to any client. "I see interior space as the scenery of everyday life."

At home, Russo's design overcomes the restricted living space by embracing and even exaggerating its limits. The bathroom reminded him of the WC in a train so he amplified its lack of space. He also resolves limits by crafting purpose-designed objects and furniture. "I am a craftsman and designer. I learned to make before I learned to design," explains Russo. Because his father was a mason, he grew up on construction sites and worked as a carpenter before studying painting and ceramics and then scenography in Florence. For five years in Berlin, he did film set and interior design and made limited-edition objects for galleries and then returned to Italy to do product design and interiors with Lissoni AssWociati and, in 2010, establish his own practice.

Today, Russo doesn't make achieving a specific style his goal; instead

> "The ambience must be a reflection of myself, mirror my equilibrium and my contradictions," he says, as he would to any client. "I see interior space as the scenery of everyday life."

clockwise:

1 The designer in front of one of the walls whose layers of paint he excavated and left unfinished to create a tissue of subtle colors over the old walls.

2 In the kitchen, the elephant drawing and the tennis racquet bowls embedded in the same wall warm the otherwise heavy concrete kitchen.

3 Russo makes many of the objects and furnishings he needs to create specific moods. This brass floor-to-ceiling shelf helped him make the most of the apartment's very limited square footage.

he begins by studying the building's cultural "aura," how it wears its history and place, and by making sketches, drawings, and collages, spurred by an existing detail or an object he has collected that may determine the mood of the entire space. "Even in a home without furniture, anyone who enters feels this aura," Russo says. "This aura is an expression of culture and should suggest the design direction." The client is not an abstraction either, but a unique person who will live in this particular space, so building and inhabitant must be suited to each other while simultaneously remaining true to themselves. In another 1930s Milan

"Found objects are like time machines, always referencing a place, person, or ambience. Disrupting their function and decontextualising them has always been a passion of mine"

building, Russo designed his brother's home, making bold-face frames from original architectural elements: deep wooden wall paneling and ceilings, a breakfast nook, and polished stone floors. He then added vintage, contemporary, or custom objects, like his bookshelf with slender diamond-shaped cross-braces, leaving plenty of open space to clarify them.

Formally, he says, it is important to maintain a geometric balance between rectangles and circles or ovals, sharp lines and soft. In his own kitchen, Russo created a softening decorative finish that brings warmth to an otherwise heavy concrete countertop that Russo envisioned as a "workbench for food." Partially scraped away wall paint, accumulated

over decades, created uneven layers of color "by causality and chance," parts of which Russo then framed: a tapestry-like section and a blushing pink and orange area that he outlined in the shape of a life-size elephant. "I like the idea that, in the past, the decoration of walls represented a certain cultural belonging," Russo says. In the same wall, he embedded tennis racquets to serve as fruit "bowls" — off-center centerpieces — whose mesh conveniently circulates air around the fruit. (He also embedded other objects in the walls, including concealed sound systems — speakers, even a carillon — that disguise the source of the sound.) "Found objects are like time machines, always referencing a place, person or ambience. Disrupting their function and decontextualising them has always been a passion of mine," he says. "In fact, I collect so many objects that they sometimes overwhelm me."

Like an old-school Italian architect, in order to create a unified, made-to-measure environment, Russo designs much of what he requires, including furniture fittings. His bathroom has a concrete sink molded in a polystyrene form that started life as packaging for mozarella cheese; its faucet is a modified garden hose. For his brother's house, he made a small brass LED lamp with an octagonal frame that can be rolled to face the light in three directions to highlight small spaces or objects that otherwise would have remained in shadow. He also created a matte black iron suspension lamp called "Metropolis," inspired by the set design of the Fritz Lang film. The source hidden in its metal structure directs light up and down while leaving the rest of the space in a penumbra.

Russo also integrates unusual authorless pieces found in flea markets or antiques stores into an interior, like the brown leather armchairs in his living room, or he cherry-picks contemporary pieces like the broad, seemingly featherweight fan-like ceiling light by Constance Guisset. Only together can the diverse furnishings contribute to the desired mood and character. "For me, what is important is the relation between objects, the composition and equilibrium or contrast they make together. My home is me in all my contradictions," Russo says. "The walls I see as a skin that protects the organs of the house, a container of meanings, so in every corner I have hidden messages for the future."

clockwise:

1 Russo preserved the original stucco, moldings, lush wood paneling and a bow window to revive the original "aura" of the house, lost during poorly executed renovations in the 1970s.

2 This diamond-trussed shelf and the Otto lamp on it were both made by Russo for the home of his brother and his wife.

3 The kitchen in the house of Russo's brother is the brightest room, a mix of eras made up of glass, wood, and fibro-cement.

4 Adriano and Silvia live in the 1930s-inflected house whose historical character Russo used as a design direction while interpreting that spirit through his own lens.

The firm's client, who works in the design industry, called the four-story townhouse his "three-dimensional business card."

Ebers Architekten built this home in the central Berlin neighborhood of Mitte, at the root of a growing arts community. The building was faced with 300,000 olive-green glass mosaic tiles and asymmetric window openings that extend from the façade at various depths. The interlocking floors also have varying ceiling heights which generate unusual sightlines—from the concrete and wood kitchen, it's possible to see much of the house—and makes its 100 sqm seem larger. Settling on a calming color throughout,

the designers used various tones of green to highlight the staircase, master bath, reading nook, and kitchen island. Capsule kids' beds built into a white wall were lined with multiple colors and a swing was hung from the living room ceiling. The project may have started out as a showcase for the client, but the designers turned it into a playground as well.

Germany // Ebers Architekten

Nuovo Mundo

Brunno Jahara's house is located in a mid-20th century building in Rio de Janeiro. Jahara conducted an experiment

in which he mixed several of his own furniture projects with objects he has gathered across the globe. He approached the interiors with great simplicity, whitewashing walls while leaving the existing exuberant colors of windows and doors—royal purple, lemon yellow, deep orange—and many original materials. It becomes an articulate and congenial mixture of folk pop with soft pastels and expressive, dark finishes: charcoal plaster walls and glossy black bathroom surfaces. Natural straw carpets and recycled wooden furniture punctuate the interiors, along with rough and tumble pieces, a bumpy resin chair and salvaged wood-plank chairs and a brightly striped credenza. Sofas and chairs were made by Jahara Studio, a combination of slender upholstered refinement and boxy blond wood. The treasure is on the balcony, however: three-legged chairs and lightly finished wooden tables made by mid-century Brazilian architect Lina Bo Bardi.

Brazil // Jahara Studio

The Maryland in Salt Lake City

The Maryland is a quirky, warm place because the combination of materials and the uniqueness of the objects inside are quirky and warm. Tiny roe deer trophy plaques are mounted to the walls and the "library" consists of a black-and-white wallcovering monolithically applied to sitting room walls. And why not? The home, in Salt Lake City, used to be an auto repair garage, so plucking objects, furnishings, and finishes out of their usual contexts was a "disorganizational" tool built into the project from the start. Designed by its owners, two salvagers and remakers of the highest order, the house is lined with stained wood surfaces that serve as a frame, but the objects framed are of a very diverse provenance. The designers repurposed found objects to make many of the furnishings and interior elements. But instead of hunting for specific objects, the couple delighted in discovering ready-mades in old military surplus stores or scrap yards and reinventing them to suit the reinvented space.

USA // Cody Derrick, Cityhome Collective

Apartment in Villefranche-sur-Mer

The open-plan design of this apartment with ocean views in Villefranche-sur-Mer uses various materials, volumes, and light to soften the boundaries between indoors and out. Referring to the sea visible outside the window, the designers applied green resin to the floors and painted the walls and ceiling white to amplify natural light. This has the effect of deepening the contrast between the blank, bright interior surfaces and other finishes. Services and private areas are contained in distinct interior volumes that do not connect to the ceiling, highlighting their function (and colored deep sea green again). MG2 designed custom furniture to personalize the space and address specific client needs. They made the central table, for instance, which they anchored to an existing concrete wall, but then they encircled it with freshly upholstered vintage seating. Garden furnishings were made to resemble interior furnishings, making the outdoors feel as much like a nest as the home inside does.

France // MG2 Architecture

Apartment in Bielmonte

The colorful Casa Andrea Zegna is a 115 sqm apartment in Bielmonte-Biella, Italy for the designer. The building in which the apartment resides was constructed during the 1960s. Zegna, whose family lived in the apartment and who spent winter holidays there until the age of 16, was keen to be as respectful as possible of its mid-century character. The designer restored a great deal of the upholstery that was original to the home while simultaneously modernizing the layout and circulation of the interiors. To this were added new wall paneling in teak and floors mosaiced in gray tiles, both matte and shiny, so that they look alternately opaque and translucent. Local carpenter Andrea Guala crafted the bookshelves and made the kitchen and wood paneling to measure. The wood floors and furniture were combined with black trim and other details, red elements like cushions and throws, and great fields of vivid green on the walls that strike a dramatic but homey contrast.

Italy // Andrea Zegna

133

Color Considered

Color Considered

Double G is a Parisian architecture, interior and furniture design studio established by Anne Geistdoerfer and Flora de Gastines in 2005. In the 9th arrondissement, the two remade the interiors of an apartment that exuded a classical Parisian ambience, and featured wooden floors and elaborate moldings. Within this classical context, the women were asked to establish a beachhead for the client's modern lifestyle and his painting and art collection. To suit the artwork, Double G painted the main rooms in basic or warm gray. Accessed by a new spiral staircase in the blue and yellow and blond wood living room, however, was doused a small upstairs library in monolithic color, every surface rendered in an invigorating but mysterious scarlet, including bookshelves and a plush red sofa. The designers added interest and animation to the house with their strategic applications of color, allowing many surfaces and objects to remain neutral, even recessive, until a shot of emotion in the form of color or pattern shakes the room awake.

France // Double G

Heavy Accents in Paris

Paris-based architecture and design firm Double G was tasked with uniting two apartments in an 18th century building in the city's first arrondissement. Though light colors—pearl gray, light blue, light green—dominate the interiors in terms of floor space, these neutral colors are punctuated irregularly with moments of robust color via furniture pieces, a window frame, graphically patterned cement tiles. Throughout, the neutral serves as a canvas for fields of strong pattern or color blocked out in measured doses: a zigzag rug against the blond wood floor, a light kitchen electrified by a fire-engine red bench and table, oak end tables with branching coral-like red legs juxtaposed with a navy rug, a single wall of unusually shaped or patterned tiles in an otherwise low-volume room. This Double G approach creates mood and character without too much fuss and no drama; instead of feeling overwhelming, the studio's interiors feel fresh, light, and carefully measured.

France // Double G

They synthesize well-known with obscure or unusual pieces by emerging talent and, often, their own bespoke items.

Studiopepe for Spotti

Multidisciplinary Milanese creative agency Studiopepe creates installations like these for Spotti Edizioni, marked by clarity, contradiction, and coherence. They may rely on a single theme, say, mirrors—hand-held, compact, tabletop, wall-mounted—or a single technique—folding, applying it to anything from kitchen furnishings to lighting—to create an interior. They synthesize well-known with obscure or unusual pieces by emerging talent and, often, their own bespoke items. In their hands, a determined color scheme is a design locomotive, not a decorative afterthought, and can supercede a room's actual structure. They use contrasts (blue with yellow, yellow with red), the monolithically monochrome (every surface yellow!) and fields of pattern (a wall of shelves filled with firewood becomes a wintry Alpine "wallcovering"). They overdo homogeneity and make connections between contraries—pairing craft with industry, the comfy and banal with the thrillingly surreal—and then glue it all together with that greatest of luxuries: empty space.

Italy // Studiopepe

Baxter

Unlike some other Italian brands, which succeed through clarity, even uniformity, of vision, Baxter has created plainly eclectic and heterogeneous collections.

What distinguishes Italian furniture producer Baxter's products, and therefore the interiors assembled from them, is the fact that it treats space as a blank page on which a story may be written to be told time and again. The protagonist of the Baxter story? Finely worked leather. The narrator? A voice that emerges from a nuanced amalgam of form, color, finishes, materials, and objects, master craftsmanship, and the most forward-looking contemporary designers. Baxter products rely heavily on hand-making and deep research to discover new, and preserve existing, craft, especially those traditions native to Italy. The company has a tradition of working with masters of design as well: Paola Navone, Matteo Thun, Draga Obradovic, and others. This has the virtue of making Baxter furnishings simultaneously specific and adaptable, expressive and versatile.

Italy // Baxter

Minotti

This particular residential scenario takes its cues—crisp forms, clean lines—from an iconic designer and a time-honored moment in contemporary American architecture:

Richard Neutra and the California Case Study Houses. Created to introduce a new furniture collection by Italian manufacturer Minotti, the interior eschews typical "contemporary" combinations of objects and furnishings, instead presenting a more engaging scenography out of the brand's furnishings. The designers established a neutral environment that nonetheless feels warm, domestic, cheerful, and chic. The occasional tables might be totems or chess pieces or oversized lathe-turned table legs and can be moved easily around the room to change it up. They also combined contrasting materials like concrete and stone with organic forms, wood, and lush upholstery. Indeed, the composition strikes an uplifting chord via a cluster of compact lounge armchairs upholstered in a jellybean jar of colors: pomegranate red, yellow, green, and raspberry. In the end, the installation could become anything from a living room to a hotel lounge or waiting room—one that you wouldn't mind waiting in at all.

Italy // Minotti

Fritz Hansen

Revered 140-year-old Danish furniture label Fritz Hansen is one of Scandinavia's lifestyle classics, associated with a Nordic aesthetic: blond wood and inviting, strong forms. Through temporary interior designs photographed for everything from its catalog to the brand's magazine, Fritz Hansen creative directors and stylists make the point that color, texture, and context are not just expressive elements, they are articulately expressive. These interior compositions, by interior designers of an unusual, ephemeral sort, form a scenography of real life. They are drawn with deep shag rugs and enamel-glazed vases. They construct scenic spaces out of driftwood, shapely glassware, a sculpture made from simple wooden dowels, nubbly upholstery in neutral tones—camels, tweeds, and charcoal are paired with cobalt blue, violet, and lemon yellow. Though ephemeral in 3D and limited to the 2D space of a photograph ever after, they stoke aspirations and become a well of inspiration.

Denmark // Fritz Hansen

Abigail Ahern

Interior designer Abigail Ahern wanted to be able to turn inward at the end of a long workday: "I wanted that gentleman's club feel whereby dark inky hues wrap you up in a cozy intriguing blanket." She used the Edwardian's ultimate refuge as a neutral, comfortable background that she deftly accessorized with doses of color, texture, and a lifetime of "oddball finds." The design is "global eclectic" because she has populated it with objects and furnishings collected over years of travel around the globe. A large blue canvas is from a gallery in LA, but two other oil paintings were flea market finds. In the living room she mixes flea market again with high-end acquisitions from auction houses. The leather chair she discovered in Paris' Porte de Vanves flea market, the sofa and pink loveseat are from George Smith. And, as she is a designer who offers others only what she herself loves, the striped zebra rug, lamps, and cushions are all available in her shop.

Vancouver House & Studio

In Vancouver's historic Gastown district, this eminently traditional, whitewashed, ivy-wrapped, 70-year-old cottage is home to eminently modern product designer Omer Arbel. Arbel, the creative director of Canadian design company Bocci, who describes himself as a tinkerer, lives with objects as he designs them. He also lives with his Weimaraner, a snake named Legs, the boa constrictor Picasso, and his girlfriend, a musician, which means creating an interior suited to living together as part of a family while maintaining space for design experimentation. The house is littered with first runs of products like his 57, 21, and 28 chandeliers, all the more beautiful for still having the kinks that were worked out of later production models. Arbel's careful choice of objects and furnishings, their casual organization and strong characters give the impression that they are quirky, eloquent housemates—modern companions in conversation with the less polished heritage house that contains them.

Canada // Omer Arbel

163

Modern Monochromy

This residential project in Paris could be represented by the work of Japanese artist Yoji Ono that is hanging in its dining room. Ono blends and abstracts classical images of art while Studio Ko has abstracted the building's details—paradoxically emphasizing its architectural origins. Built at the turn of the 18th and 19th centuries as a 7th arrondissement hotel particulier, its bourgeois history is still visible in the original architecture: marble fireplaces, mirrored glass in gilt frames, wooden wall paneling and the portes dérobée or invisible doors hidden in it; a 4.5-meter high ceiling and herringbone oak floorboards were all called back into service by the architects. The organization of the rooms was maintained. Master craftsmen were commissioned to make furnishings and the designers established a "monochrome" approach to each room, rendering each in a slightly different shade. The goal was to breathe new life into the antique box by enabling it to contain a contemporary lifestyle and décor.

France // Studio Ko

Milano Solferino

Dimore Studio composed the interior of this 18th-century Milanese palazzo with a cool color palette and seamlessly rendered temporal mash-ups. The designers imagined the palazzo, with its high vaulted ceilings, as "a container for contemporary life" that would house objects curated from indeterminate times and places while establishing contemporary moments. In sum, these generate a palpable sense of both texture and timelessness. The designers submerged the interiors in "a color of historical importance," a shade of blue with undertones of gray and green whose hue seems to shift with the quality of natural light. Light filters sparingly through the imposing original architecture, allowing the composition of a dramatic scenography, a cool underwater world. The Dimore designers deftly layered color and materials — silk rugs with oxidized metals and wood that wears its age proudly. In the kitchen, they juxtaposed a late 18th-century Gustavian day bed with a new brass-clad island of their own design and a wooden cupboard from a Piemonte sacristy that recalls an old altar. >>

>> The salon features a Verner Panton luster, artwork made from recycled cement, a Chinese Art Deco rug, and a contemporary armchair, along with a 17th-century church altarpiece. In the dining room, a vintage Kartell pedant lives with a marble Saarinen dining table and Gio Ponti's Superleggera chairs. In new contexts and combinations, the objects assume new identities and forge unexpected associations. Their interleaving renders the interiors more human in scale while retaining a sense of the palazzo's original grandeur and gravity.

Italy // Dimore Studio

Dimore Studio

Interior and Furniture Designers // Milan, Italy

Points of View

Among the photographs in Dimore Studio's interior design portfolio are fragments of images—the shadow of an unseen palm tree across the blue cushion of a lounge chair, a cloud of peonies tumbling from a colorless cluster of glazed ceramic jugs—details emblematic of the Milan studio's emotionally immersive work. Emiliano Salci and Britt Moran are curators, scenographers, historians, collectors, portraitists, and a couple whose interiors represent the simultaneously rigorous and poetic expression of two unique points of view. Seen through their lens, space is a collage of times and places that forms a darkly glamorous here and now. They layer objects, materials and colors, synthesize historical periods and cultivate complex moods the way a perfumer blends the notes of a new fragrance.

Salci grew up in a Tuscan farmhouse. Moran has as mixed a provenance as the objects that fill their interiors. Born in North Carolina, he studied in Edinburgh and has long lived in Europe. The couple, who came from art direction (Salci), graphic design (Moran) and home furnishings (both)

met while working on a Shanghai hotel and now share a 17th-century villa in Brera above their ground floor studio where their commissions include hotels and restaurants, furniture, shops and homes.

Through their editing and composition of interior still lifes, they fill space while making it feel coherent and spare. They avoid the superfluous and the provocative, but their work is deeply atmospheric, consisting of an intriguing imbalance of extremes—dramatic and serene, enigmatic and forthright, plain and sophisticated. This approach suited the design of Milan restaurant Ceresio 7 where the menu consists of unconventional combinations of simple ingredients. In the washroom, an Asian-inflected wallcovering depicts leaves that become a forest when multiplied in a series of mirrors hung at an angle to the wall and in the mirrored ceiling above. The diffuse light of the ceiling lamp suggests the moon and below it, like abstracted lanterns, hang two brass wall sconces.

"To give character to a space, we like objects with special details that are not immediately evident," says Salci. "The object itself may be hidden or it may have some hidden preciousness that isn't apparent at first sight, but which will be discovered on closer examination." A 300-year-old table, for instance, may appear to be "just a very nice table," but closer inspection may

> "To give character to a space, we like objects with special details that are not immediately evident," says Salci. "The object itself may be hidden or it may have some hidden preciousness that isn't apparent at first sight."

The "stories" that these relationships suggest have no beginning, middle or end, but they are felt and understood, like music, both viscerally and emotionally.

reveal an elaborate mother-of-pearl inlay. Their juxtapositions, however, mean that nothing old ever feels worn, just lush: tarnished metals, silk rugs and wood worn by time the way driftwood is worn by water coexist with new bespoke objects, Chinese Art Deco and mid-century modern furnishings. Often they find a piece and only later discover a use for it. They once transformed two weight plates from an old scale into a pair of wall lights.

Their work may represent couture-level luxury, but it is the luxury of living with stories and histories, not merely a luxury of things. It is not single objects that make a space, Salci explains: "What really counts is the interaction each object has with those surrounding it." By placing objects and furniture in new contexts and combinations, Salci and Moran generate unanticipated links—and start conversations—among them. In Solferino, a home in an 18th-century palazzo, a painted daybed, a brass-clad island and a humble wooden

altar seem to share the same spirit. We don't know what the conversations are about, only that each object affects the others and becomes something more in their company—rather the way people do in their own relationships.

Color and texture do part of the story-telling too: The designers' own living room is a pelagic blue-green-gray lifted from an old painting to create a real-life chiaroscuro. They either use big fields of color that appear to contain many colors or vivid, saturated, unmistakable hues as punctuation. And, by affinity or contrast, colors lead the eye to colors and shapes to shapes. In their St. Germain project, the children's bedroom contains blue animal print curtains, blue wallpaper, a glazed navy vase—and, beside them, a scarlet bed frame. In the dining room, soft globes illuminate a room fractured with geometric shards: a striped wooden dining table, a puzzle of triangular wooden tiles, a sharply rectangular fireplace. The living room chandelier

is an angular sculpture of brass stems and bare bulbs that echoes the angular honeycomb pattern of the David Hicks carpet below, but the carpet's angles lead the eye to the soft crescent of the red couch, the color of which leads to the red palm tree drapes, the pattern of which leads to a palm frond floor lamp. The "stories" that these relationships suggest have no beginning, middle or end, but they are felt and understood, like music, both viscerally and emotionally.

Not least, Salci and Moran consider light essential in shaping and making space versatile. As Salci points out, light serves as a partition without requiring any wall. They use a variety of lights in combination or alone—warm light, not cold, because it brings out colors, textures and materials—to make space adaptable to any given mood or function. (They also prefer old lampshades—made from linen, silk, parchment or tinplate—because they diffuse light in a "charismatic" way.)

Previous spread (left to right):

1 Britt Moran (left) and Emiliano Salci are Dimore Studio.

2 Colors lead the eye to colors and shapes to shapes in the living room of the St. Germain residence in Paris.

This spread (clockwise):

1 One of the many scenic patterns and color combinations in the St. Germain, Paris residence.

2 The restroom in the Ceresio 7 restaurant in Milan suggests a forest.

3+4 Rich materials, like marble for the fireplace, grainy wood and buttery leather, signal comfort at Ceresio 7.

Light was crucial in Solferino, where the palazzo's dim vaulted ceilings might have swallowed the living space, if not for a lighting scheme that privileged the human scale and the lush eye-level scenography. As much as the illumination, Salci and Moran consider the shade cast by light. Which goes back to that odd fragment of a photograph included in their portfolio: a photo not of the lounge chair they chose for the pool deck and not of the palm tree swaying above it, but of the shadow that one casts over the other, an ordinary, extraordinary pattern that will change at every moment of every day.

Franklin Street Loft

As one might expect from a Nordic studio, natural materials are key to Copenhagen (and New York) based Søren Rose Studio's work, partly because they are abundant and partly because they grow more beautiful with age. The oak tree, for instance, is common throughout Scandinavia, and is used copiously in Rose's furniture and interior design work. It also sits well with the birch plank floor that stretches across the open-plan TriBeCa residential loft in Manhattan. Rose used oil-rubbed American white oak and white laminate to make the living room sofa, as well as the TriBeCa desk (part of a larger collection created especially for this project). Also part of the TriBeCa collection, the lamp unites brass, ceramic, and glass while the kitchen table comprises a slab of marble. A number of chairs in the loft— dining chairs reupholstered in Kvadrat fabric, and an Eames chair—are vintage. In Rose's organic-looking environment, the natural materials and aged pieces co-exist, well, naturally.

USA // Søren Rose Studio

The Tree Top Chalet

The Tree Top Chalet is a private home that exemplifies one way in which the design of an interior can be predicated on its surroundings. It also highlights Rose's commitment to honest materials. The so-called Chalet crowns a hill in Vejby, Denmark, and, guarded by woods, is what Rose calls a "natural haven." Rose's design team used the green-hued, wood-parodying WrongWoods credenza from Established & Sons and smoked or oiled oak on the floor and in cabinetry to bring the outdoors inside. In fact, oak is ubiquitous from the flooring and millwork to the furniture. The kitchen lamps by Tom Dixon, hammered from reflective brass, suggest earth tones while a traditional wood-burning stove makes reference to the simplicity of living close to nature. The studio itself sewed the Harlequin bed throw from salvaged Kvadrat fabrics. Rose provided counterpoint to the fresh, blank white walls and black details that imbue the space with calm by providing moments of color that inject both energy and strong character.

Denmark // Søren Rose Studio

Tünel Residence

Istanbul-based Autoban blends its robustly refined, taste-making aesthetic with history and humorous quirks in its scheme for the Tünel Residence. The 190 sqm apartment sits on the ground floor of the 19th-century Hamson building in Beyoğlu at a tranquil distance from the buzzing alleys and touristed streets of Tünel. Autoban found the apartment in poor condition and with a senseless layout, inhibiting circulation, and affected repairs, altering the plan, for instance, to extend the living areas, kitchen, and master bath. A long parquet pattern and black and white coats of paint embellish the floors and offer a counterpoint to the exposed brickwork. The client's personality was expressed in the dark palette of black, gray and walnut as well as a kitchen tailored to his frequent cooking. Its white tiles, whitewashed brick and an opulent pressed metal ceiling enlarge the small, windowless space and are topped with the studio's own Flying Spider chandelier. Custom tiles typical of old Istanbul homes wrap the bathroom and WC in timeless patterns. In the living room, the studio's two-seater Deco Sofa is paired with an Eames lounger and bouquet-like sconces inspired by fixtures found in nearby antique shops. It is a playful interweaving of traditional elements with new Autoban pieces that brings together the rich visual culture of Istanbul's past and the burgeoning modernity that is springing from its fertile ground.

Turkey // Autoban

Opera Palas

Opera Palas

Despite the rather grand name of the Opera Palas building, it was designed by an opera lover only 45 years ago and then used, rather prosaically, as an office. Autoban's intervention in the Istanbul apartment was predicated on the creation of an "undecorated" space. It features daylight as the primary design element to create a space that is not prosaic at all. Eschewing decoration, Autoban's design was heavily influenced by functionality and the lifestyle of its inhabitant, who works in the design and art businesses, and who needed clean, uncluttered space in which to display his product prototypes and artwork. To begin, the team stripped away the extraneous accumulations of years—walls, partitions, layers of paint—to reduce the space to its most basic elements. Then they started fresh, with a white cube that became the project's canvas and using a palette of basic geometric shapes. The client's library of books were then not just stored but displayed in four elliptical Autoban bookcases and juxtaposed with furniture classics by Ray and Charles Eames and George Nakashima to form a study. The rest of the interiors feature the studio's own prototypes, including an early Box sofa, and the Pebble and Cloud tables.

Turkey // Autoban

Autoban

Architect & Interior Designer // Istanbul, Turkey

At the Crossroads of Old & New

marble, along with Turkey's deeply authentic and storied visual culture. "Layers make the space more rich," says Özdemir. "You can read very clearly the materials and ideas in layered spaces." When working with a historical building or apartment, they strip everything superfluous away to reveal the most remarkable details. Their multilayered approach allows them to visualize and make palpable every period of the space's existence and to create a visible timeline of its history. There are times when they uncover, say, frescoes, only to find that they may be too damaged to restore. Either they leave them as-is, or they hunt down the right person to fix or complete them. "It is the building or apartment that tells you when to stop," Özdemir explains.

If they discover a detail from the history of the building, they will elaborate on it, but they will not insert a detail that wasn't already there. In their Beyoglu residence, part of the ceiling was missing, but the designers wanted to restore the building's original patterns. After searching, they found the plaster mold for that pattern in a local workshop not far from the apartment, kept by a craftsman who has also archived patterns from Dolmabahçe Palace.

In preserving these original features, they use them as backgrounds for contemporary living. The starting point for the design of the first sensibly modern House Café was the former family home in Nisantasi where the café is located. Autoban told a story about the richness of traditional Turkish family life through various objects and materials: wooden spindle-back benches or crystal chandeliers. "We are

For all the modernity of their interiors, the work of Istanbul's Autoban design studio is defined by its intriguing reconciliation of old and new. An architect and interior designer, respectively, former university classmates Seyhan Özdemir and Sefer Çağlar founded Autoban in 2003. At first, their interiors layered new, bespoke elements around the best bits of a meticulously preserved historical shell. Within several years, however, the layers—not just of time periods, but forms, materials, and ideas—would become more numerous and less bifurcated, their interleaving more nuanced and complex.

Although it may be a challenge to work in Istanbul's much-partitioned buildings, the city more than makes up for this with its wealth of patterns, textures and histories. Özdemir and Çağlar privilege authentic materials: walnut, brass,

> "Layers make the space more rich, you can read very clearly the materials and ideas in layered spaces." When working with a historcal building or apartment, they strip everything superfluous away to reveal the most remarkable details.

clockwise:

1 Seyhan Özdemir (left), architect, and Sefer Çağlar (right), interior designer, met as university classmates and founded Autoban in 2003.

2 The café in the Savoy Ulus Club House with its faceted oak and maple plank shell, which lends a human scale to the cavernous building it nests in.

3 The House Hotel Galatasaray layers geometric patterns with traditional details.

4 Autoban preserved the classical 19th-century Zenovich townhouse in which the Galatasaray hotel is located and mined it for inspiration and original architectural elements.

"A home should tell about the lifestyle and the personality of the people who live in it. One should be surrounded by the things that one is interested in and inspired by, that nourish your interests on creative and intellectual levels."

storyteller-architects," says Özdemir. "With the layering system, there is a story already existing and then we create a story." The space becomes, not a blend, but a dovetailing of those stories.

For a residential commission in Tünel, they had to work with a space that was nearly derelict, only vestiges of its halcyon days recoverable: the wooden floor, fragments of ceiling frescoes, and tall, double-hung wooden window frames. "We needed to imagine the rest of it to complete the picture, and add just what needed to be added," she says. "What we did was to adapt its features to today's way of living." The kitchen was very small, so they converted one of the extra rooms into a kitchen and turned the original kitchen into a storage unit. They exposed the brick walls, kept the ceiling above the corridor as it was found, and reproduced the traditional tiles to showcase the property's past as a frame for contemporary furnishings, including Emeco chairs and the studio's own Box sofa and a few antique store finds like a loveseat that they restored, repainted, and re-upholstered.

Found objects come from almost anywhere from secondhand furniture

shops to flea markets. Once they found a Herman Miller chair that had been left on the kerb and used it in their Mısır Apartment loft. The starting point for their Spider lamp was an object they got from one of the junk dealers who sells his wares on the street from a wheelbarrow. Often, however, they will combine the historical pieces will design classics, custom furniture, or items from their own growing product collection. In the Opera Palas

apartment, the studio's Cloud Table was combined with chairs by George Nakashima or the Castiglioni brothers' pendant lamp Taraxacum 88.

Autoban usually develops its concept of a space—through sketches and moodboards initially and then CAD and, more extensively, 3D models—based on the character, history, or function of the original space, but, if it is devoid of worthwhile details, they will create their own "second shell" inside. They designed an irregular second shell inside the Savoy Ulus Club House, a mixed-use sports and entertainment center inside an asymmetrical, avant-garde architectural compound whose structure was dictated largely by the site's varying grade. In a constant negotiation with the larger structure, Autoban's micro-architectural approach nested a shell of new forms, materials, textures, and patterns within the first shell. The faceted oak and maple-plank shell establishes a human scale within the cavernous building that alternately supports and divorces itself from its surfaces. "We always keep a gap between the original building and the layers we add," says Özdemir. Sometimes it's a literal gap: In their restaurant Gaspar, the interior membrane built into the existing envelope is mounted anywhere from 20 cm to almost a meter away from the original structure.

Always, the goal of the narrative Autoban create with an interior is to offer its occupant a new experience: "A home should tell about the lifestyle and the personality of the people who live in it. One should be surrounded by the things that one is interested in and inspired by, that nourish your interests on creative and intellectual levels and provide the space for their pursuit," Özdemir explains. "We believe that the furniture and other components of a home will shape its owner's mood and quality of life."

"We believe that the furniture and other components of a home will shape its owner's mood and quality of life."

clockwise:

1 The Ayazpaşa apartment features a bathroom paying homage to the traditional marble hamam but in a contemporary spirit.

2 The Witt Suites Hotel is a chic showcase for the studio's growing furniture and product collection.

3 The identity of the House Hotel Bosphorus was largely predicated on the historical building in which it is located, even while it is full of the most modern furnishings.

4 Gaspar is a box within a historical architectural box. Based on knolling, the collage of wood panels forming the interior box hang anywhere from 20 cm to one meter from the original walls.

Hervé Van der Straeten Apartment

Taking advantage of a whole-building renovation, French artist and designer Hervé Van der Straeten reinvented his 19th-century loft and former studio as a living space with an emphasis on graphical forms, striking materials, and unconventional compositions inspired by light. Van der Straeten knocked down walls, laid polished concrete floors, and partitioned the open space with heavy camel-colored curtains (scarlet in the bedroom). Many of the furnishings, lighting and artworks are Van der Straeten's, forms that are architectural or sculpted and sensually finished with lacquer, wood, bronze, and gold leaf. But his work finds a counterpoint in that of others. His collection mixes antiques with the avant-garde and plastic forms with craftsmanship. The living room features a Danish sofa, tables by Pierre Charpin, and a large mobile. Beside the classical fireplace mantel, leather armchairs by English designer Jasper Morrison sit beside five-legged Louis XV seats. Elsewhere, a Louis XVI sofa is flanked by Bouroullec brother chairs while van der Straeten's Capsule stool accompanies a Pierre Paulin armchair.

France // Hervé Van der Straeten

Hervé Van der Straeten Apartment

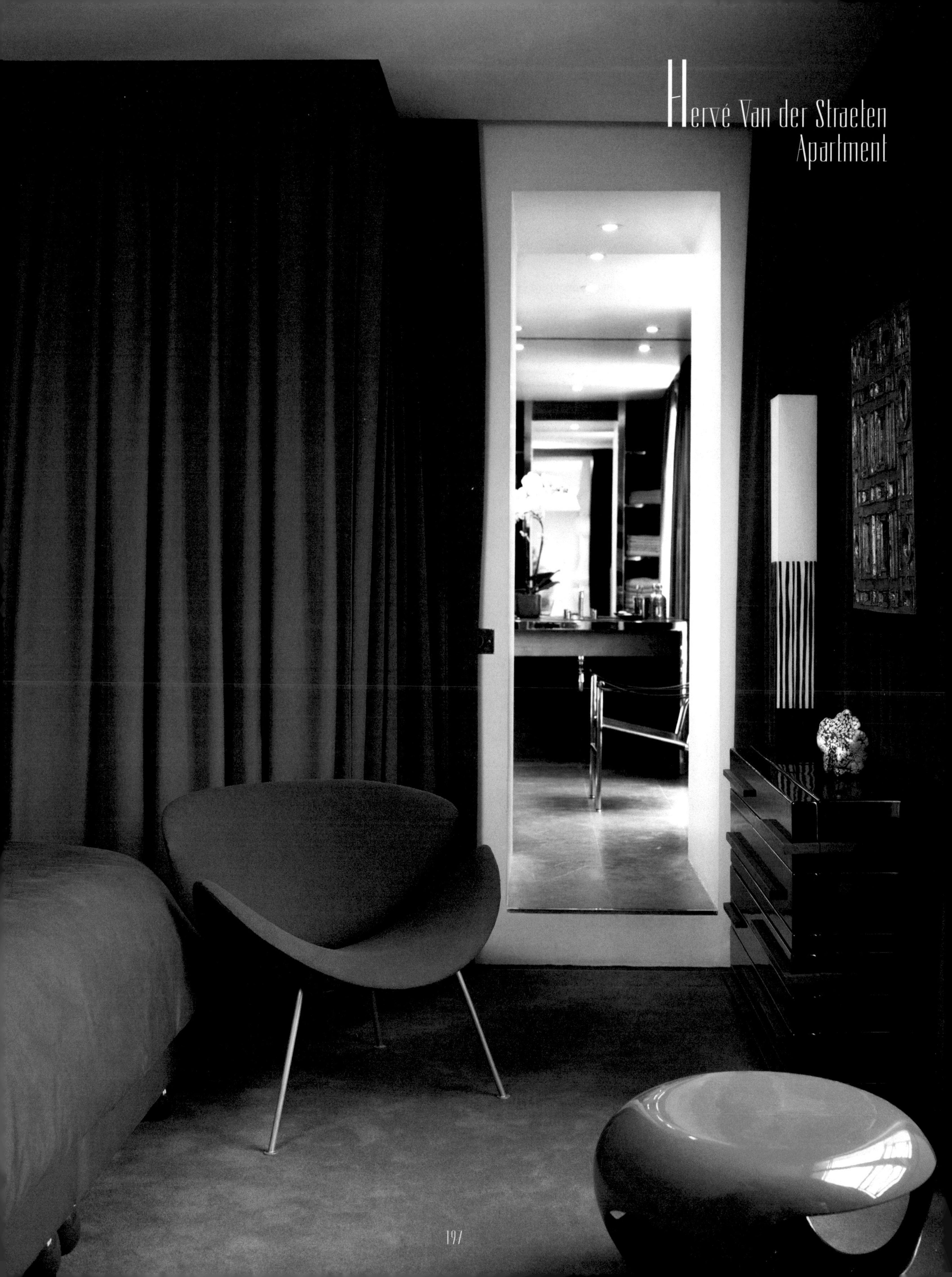

A riad, from the Arabic for garden, is a vernacular Moroccan house defined by its interior garden or courtyard.

Dar Emma

The architecture of Dar Emma, located in the Marrakech medina, was comprehensively rehabilitated to declare its Moroccan provenance explicitly: Owners Emma Rochlitzer and Roberto Caciolli preserved or reproduced elements, using tadelakt, an almost waterproof lime plaster, concrete walls and floors, stone from Ouarzazate in Marocco for the patio, the original wood and stucco ceilings, typical columns, and heavy carved doors. Meanwhile, the interiors and furniture convey the inhabitants' European origins and lifestyle through imported chandeliers and mirrors from Murano, vintage chairs and tables from the 1950s to the 1970s, family heirlooms, and souvenirs from travels, including sculptures, African masks, and antique Chinese cabinets. They ensured that the mix of classic furniture with authorless old pieces found in Paris galleries and Moroccan flea markets would create a mash-up of visual cultures that suits them uniquely.

Morocco // Emma Rochlitzer, Roberto Caciolli

Shinsuke Kawahara Apartment in Paris

Japanese artist, fashion, product, and interior designer Shinsuke Kawahara's Paris apartment is a variegated terrain inhabited by rabbits—porcelain rabbits, silver Christofle rabbits, wooden rabbits from 1915, rabbit bags, and rabbit lawn ornaments. In this landscape, the clutter is topographical, mapping out routes and destinations and consists of stacked books, a variety of seating, shots of color—a complex and engrossing story about who Kawahara is. He preserved the original 17th-century architectural elements—chevron hardwood flooring, a wooden arch, exposed ceiling beams, and a fireplace and built a tea-room-within-the-living-room. Interleaved eras and styles, contrasting patterns and textures, this shrine to purposeful eclecticism looks as if it were the result of an organic process, occurring over time, which because he is a traveler and collector, it did. Kawahara has a special appreciation for unique handmade objects—they improve with age, just as a home and the person who lives there should.

France // Shinsuke Kawahara

Eric Goode Loft

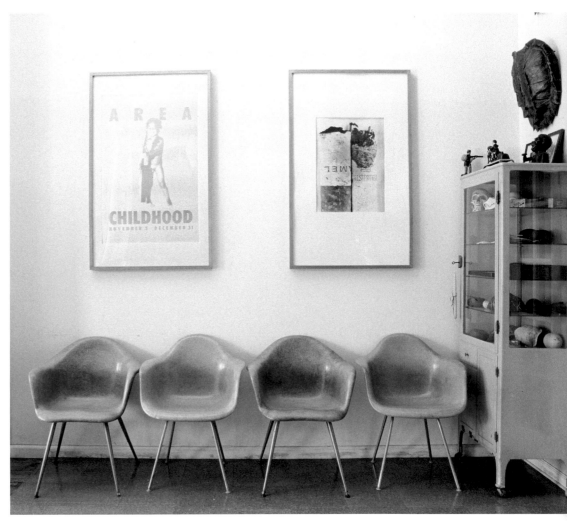

The design of this industrial Noho penthouse in New York for artist and former 1980s nightclub impresario Eric Goode had a hard act or two to follow.

Goode owned the legendary Area club, which regularly hosted installations by Goode's cronies like artists Andy Warhol, Keith Haring, and Jean-Michel Basquiat. His next club, MK, was designed as a fictional house. Goode's loft, designed by Goode himself, is just as unconventional if not as grandiose. It is filled with taxidermied animals who died from natural causes: a vintage stuffed lion and a Midwestern bulldog who was freeze-dried for six months before being stuffed by Preserve a Pet. These real life "sculptures" live amidst items like Chinese lanterns, a Le Corbusier sofa, and a drawer of human bones, whose owner may or may not have died from natural causes. Color explodes throughout the house in big blocks or details. In the lemon yellow kitchen, the fridge is Yves Klein blue. The rest of the house's color is provided by the artworks of celebrities of those halcyon days like photographer Nan Goldin—which are very colorful indeed.

USA // Eric Goode

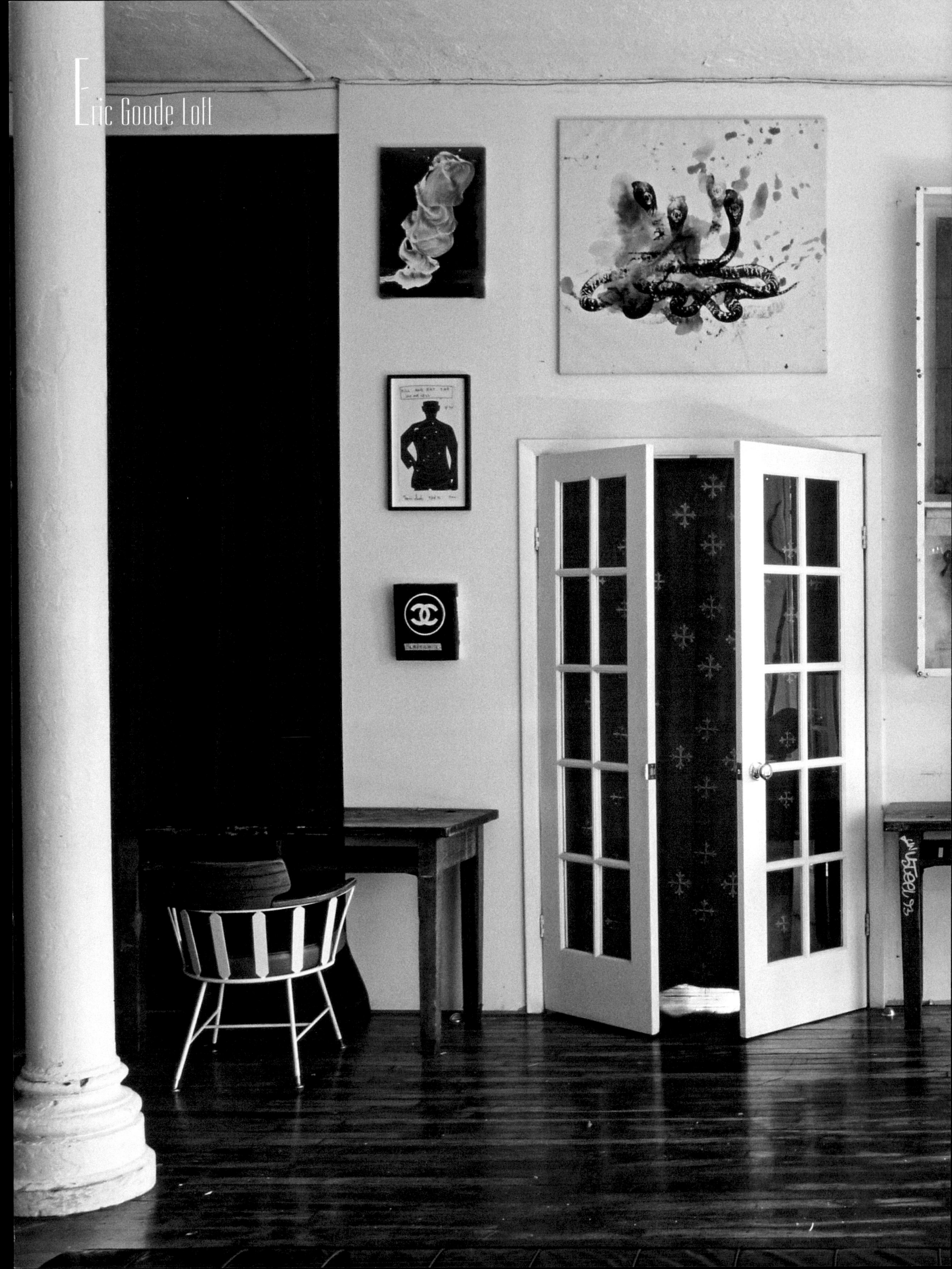

Eric Goode Loft

George Koukourakis House in Nisyros

Architect George Koukourakis restored this 120-year-old residence on the Greek island of Nisyros for himself. He honored the history of the155 sqm home while updating it with stylistic or historic contrasts and a contrasting color scheme. First, he preserved the house's original cement tile flooring and restored wooden elements like the staircase and closets. He generated a ranging color palette starting with the house's original red oxide and assigned a color to each room based on function, using more dynamic hues in public spaces: the dining room is bright green, the kitchen canary yellow. He pulled the color of the ceiling down over cabinets and other elements in a single block, even applying it to an antique stove, combining the bold contemporaneity of the color to a traditional object. In the bedrooms, aside from the iron rosette beds, the furniture is spare, striking contrasts between old and new, ornate and bare, that in his hands become harmonious.

Greece // George Koukourakis

Rungstedgaard Hotel

For this hotel and conference space in a rehabilitated 1917 manor house, designer Frederikke Aagaard chose modern colors, lighting, and furniture, but retained the finest bits of the original architectural envelope. From the start, she preserved elements like blond wood parquet floors, the graphical but austere stair railings, a florid fireplace mantel, and the building's original electrical brass chandelier, which resembles a piece of antique jewelry. Paintings she found, along with an old kilim rug, in the hotel's stores and hung them with art, ceramic and metal objects, mirrors, and lamps found in antique shops. Then she fitted the historical shell with modern pieces by the likes of Jaime Hayon and the Bouroullec brothers, avoiding sturdy but cliché hotel furnishings. Unexpectedly, by bringing in carefully considered contemporary design, the designer was able to shine a light on the building's legacy.

Denmark // Frederikke Aagaard

Notting Hill House

Notting Hill house is a blend of North African, Victorian, and modern sensibilities and is personalized with objects found during the architect's travels. Kassar constructed platforms in the house and preserved the clarity of the lines that define existing spaces. Though the team retained parquet flooring and the arc of the original balustrade, they also gave height to the interiors by demolishing small corridors that had broken them up and eliminated partitions from the lower levels. This allowed Kassar to create larger, multipurpose rooms around the library's central void. Textural details provide visual richness and the human scale that had been lacking due to the extreme narrowness of the structure. A narrow terrace and steel kitchen with an uneven mirrored ceiling are both tiled in a pattern of gray tones. Craftsmanship gave new life to materials like tile, mirror, and wood, but also explored modern techniques for fabricating them.

UK // Annabel Kassar

Pittsburgh Loft

Designer Stacy Weiss of Studio Weisshouse made her Pittsburgh home her own through lovingly collected furniture and artwork. Weiss trolls for these defining elements at furniture dealers and flea markets, on the internet, in antique stores, and through barters with artists. She buys nothing for a client that she wouldn't put in her own home, she says, but sometimes Weiss can't bring herself to give something away. Instead, she puts it in her own home where objects are arranged without hierarchy. The dressing room features a heritage dress form, work by outside artist Karl Mullen, and a throw knitted by her daughter. In the bedroom, vintage artwork hangs above an area rug by Virgil Cantini. The desk in the guest room is an old Herman Miller design and, elsewhere, she puts a Turkish rug with a Noguchi lamp, a B&B Italia armchair, and an Indonesian sculpture. A Saarinen dining table stands near an authorless Ottoman that she inherited from her parents. Gathered together, these pieces make Weiss' house a home that is surely greater than the sum of its parts.

USA // Stacy Weiss

Our Historic Apartment

Kelee Katillac's interiors are layered with inspiration, allusions and images composed as if for the cinema or stage. Where some interiors draw on a single concept, Katillac's are "ensemble" productions, uniting objects of divergent provenance without them looking miscast or garbled. She based the design of this apartment on romantic archetypes and jewel tones, mining her gemstone collection to find the hue that would dominate each room: blue chalcedony, amethyst, sulphur yellow, rose quartz, and aquamarine. She invokes archetypes and cultural icons from literature, film, art, history, and music to create backstories for design elements. The mid-20th century master bedroom is aquamarine and neo-classical, featuring objects recalling Hollywood Regency, Oscar Wilde, and the Algonquin Hotel. Can an interior become a compass in life? By representing these icons in her home, Katillac says, she has been absorbing daily the very qualities that made them so inspirational.

USA // Kelee Katillac

218

Apartment Refurbishment in Consell de Cent

Anna and Eugeni Bach fit this Barcelona apartment together like a jigsaw puzzle. In this oft-renovated, 100-year-old building, only some original joinery, the rosette and molding-clad ceilings, and old hydraulic paving floors had survived intact, and most of the designers' alterations avoided these historical elements. The designers recessed wardrobes or shifted partitions to enlarge the space while using the generous ceiling height to elevate the bath-room floor, tucking in storage, and adding three steps up to the bedroom. They lined the hallway with shelving and suspended Ikea tabletop lamps upside-down from the ceiling to provide focused light and a sense of surreality, so that within the clean and the modern, an unconventional character emerged.

Spain // Anna & Eugeni Bach

Cape of Good Hope House

French photographer Jean-Marc Lederman bought this house on the Cape of Good Hope in South Africa for its unrivaled view—and then renovated and designed it himself. Although the structure was rather work-a-day and demanded a deep renovation, it was situated on a rocky headland 150 km away from the southernmost tip of the African continent, with all of the visual drama that its location would seem to imply. Before he began the three-year renovation, Lederman lived in the house for a year, noting every shift of light through days and seasons. Lederman excavated the original ceiling beams, peeled off much of their accumulated paint layers and left them unfinished, juxtaposed with the bare concrete walls of the living room and the stone chimney. Hung with canvases and sculptures, it is a gallery of both art and design and a mash-up of time periods. From the infinity pool, however, the view remains timeless.

South Africa / Jean-Marc Lederman

225

The Harmony Club

This 1,858 sqm waterfront building in sleepy Selma, Alabama was built in 1909 as a social club and lay abandoned for nearly 40 years before industrial designer David Hurlbut bought it. Hurlbut saw it as his own private clubhouse and, over the course of two years, did most of the renovation work himself, preserving the whispered histories of the old architecture. Hurlbut describes the aesthetic as "neo-Gilded Age steampunk," "neo-Edwardian," and "castle-y" but the interiors pair a haunted southern gothic beauty with the nonchalance of the old-time men's club. Hurlbut exposed layers of the walls and left them unfinished, trapping flakes of peeling paint or paper under light coats of polyurethane paint like bugs in amber. In one bathroom, he kept a white-tiled shower but mounted a big crucifix to the wall. At auctions, he found big furnishings that would not be diminished by the vastness of the rooms. The Harmony Club is an ongoing project, Hurlbut says gleefully. He may never be done.

USA // David Hurlbut

David Hurlbut

Industrial Designer and Architectural Consultant // Selma, USA

The Harmony Club

The Harmony Club is called The Harmony Club not because owner and designer David Hurlbut is very comfortable living in it (although he is), but because that's what the businessmen called it who built it as a social club in Selma, Alabama a century ago. And Hurlbut, whose life has been consumed with restoring, updating and making it his own for the past several years and will be for the foreseeable future, believes in keeping all the good bits of an historical structure that he can. That's what he tells his clients too: Leave as much of the original structure intact as you can. Strip away elements that are not true to the original architecture but have accumulated over the years. Get down to the bones of the

place, but don't erase any of the accumulated spirit with which being lived in for so long has invested it.

Hurlbut was born and raised in Atlanta, Georgia, which, before the 1996 Summer Olympics arrived, was an undiscovered "playground of architecture," he recalls. "I ran with a like-minded group of friends who would explore abandoned warehouses and skate desperate alleys." So after graduating from Georgia Tech in industrial design, it made sense that he began to buy property around Atlanta, and later other Southern states, to renovate and put back on the market.

The last project Hurlbut finished was in Atlanta where he was working as an architectural consultant and industrial designer. For that restoration, he added an HVAC system — sympathetically, without altering the building's character — and then turned some French doors into windows. "I took an early 19th-century grocery store and turned it into an urban fortress," he explains. "My aesthetic has a rough glimmer; I like the look of a slightly polished gem."

But how does he decide how much polish is enough polish but not too much? How does he choose when to leave something as is and when to remake or replace it? At which layer does he stop excavating paint layers on a wall? The answer is that Hurlbut works with what he's got, ensures it's structurally sound and, if something is beyond repair, removes it but leaves the area where the dysfunctional bit was excised, exposed. It's like honoring the wound by wearing the scar.

When it came to furniture, Hurlbut had the vast ceilings and grand architectural elements to contend with: "I realized quickly that I had to think large on furnishings," he admits, "because this place swallows furniture."

"Sometimes there are big roof repairs and then other days, its just a good vacuuming, that does the trick," he says. "Living in the restoration is heaven for me."

The paint on the walls of the Harmony Club today is original layers, which were only a few layers deep in the first place. When he moved into the building, Hurlbut took a broom and swept the peeling paint off, leaving whatever the brisk sweeping he'd given it couldn't sweep away. "The process has left a beautiful mosaic of paint chips," he says. "Now the walls could be photographed and made into a wallpaper pattern." He also upgraded the electrical system, but when it was turned on, the original knob and tube system were functioning, so he kept them and, in concession to them, simply runs very low-wattage light bulbs. The bright side of living with illumination that could practically be measured in candles? It transports Hurlbut into the house's low-wattage past.

When it came to furniture, Hurlbut had the vast ceilings and grand architectural elements to contend with: "I realized quickly that I had to think large on furnishings," he admits, "because this place swallows furniture." He hunted down big old pieces that turned out to be cheap because people didn't have the room to store them anymore.

After that, the choice of objects came down to Hurlbut's singular tastes: "I prefer to live with older pieces, taxidermied creatures and amber light bulbs," he says. He lists, as his "style mentors," the creepy-comic geniuses of black humor: Edward Gorey and Charles Addams. Which explains a lot. Whether he believes in ghosts or not, Hurlbut is certainly not afraid of them. He loves objects that are "haunted"

with stories and histories. In fact, if a home is too sterile — because it's trendy or conforms to aesthetic conventions thought to be "safe," Hurlbut admits to feeling a little anxious. He wants to get a feel for who someone is when he visits their home, but that requires a point of view and the will to state it. Which is why Hurlbut is amused by extreme minimalism. "A home should first entertain its owner and then the owner's guests," he says, "and if the guests are not entertained, they can be ushered politely to the door without too much resistance."

What this means is that after Hurlbut recovers the bones of a building, what he adds is what suits his Gorey tastes. He bought the gargoyle above his bed and made molds from it, to cast replicas for

"A home should first entertain its owner and then the owner's guests," he says, "and if the guests are not entertained, they can be ushered politely to the door without too much resistance."

use around the house and hung the façade with four busts that he'd sculpted from wet cement. At times he will even use inexpensive Halloween masks to cast these fantastical pieces.

The Harmony Club is not finished, which may be because Hurlbut has been having far too much fun not finishing it. On the one hand, this level of historical patina is something that cannot be bought in a store, but on the other, he also doesn't want to simply return it to the way it looked at its beginning. Restoration is a day-by-day work-in-progress—even a passion-in-progress—that Hurlbut relishes in a funny work-a-day way: "Sometimes there are big roof repairs and then other days its just a good vacuuming, that does the trick," he says. "Living in the restoration is heaven for me."

The metamorphosis of this 1852 home in Hopefield, South Africa, into a guest house began with no plumbing and bad recent additions like a conservatory made of green plastic sheeting.

Laurent Bayard preserved the original windows and Oregon pine flooring and brought back original period elements, using carreaux cement flooring, antique brass fittings and Victorian tubs for two of the bathrooms, for example. But he added contemporary items like a plexiglass coffee table, a Paco Rabanne-inspired wall, a Sean Connery cushion paired with a gray flannel chair. Bayard has also designed bags, jewelry, houses, and gardens according to different styles and periods (his grandfather conserved antique paintings). The living room is filled with the artifacts of 30 years of living and traveling in Europe, India, and Morocco in markets, flea markets, antique fairs, and museums. And then there's the room of stuffed animals—which is a reminder that sometimes design details are worth a thousand words.

South Africa // Laurent Bayard

239

Ny Townhouse Conversion

Eclectic reigns in this townhouse converted by The New Design Project and its creative director Fanny Abbes. The designers started by painting walls monolithically gray and white to de-emphasize period features like wall moldings and to make the mood more youthful. Abbes made of each room a plain, neutral box and then layered the styles of various eras within, punctuating these layers emphatically with color and contrast. The effect is to take the pretention out of what could have been a historical shell with too much gravity and inject some good-looking levity. To cultivate this eclecticism, Abbes' team salvaged and repurposed objects from thrift shops, antique dealers, ordinary retail, and custom orders. In every space, there is a sense of asymmetry and texture expressed through confrontations among objects. In the living and dining room, a lime green armchair collides with a 1980s-invoking hot pink lacquered coffee table while both of these face-off with historical hand-drawn portraits, a mid-century modern walnut credenza, and a traditional marble mantelpiece. Also in the dining room, a Technicolor vintage travel print overlooks a serene vignette of wooden furnishings from the 1960s. These self-conscious contrasts don't feel awkward or cluttered because Abbes constructed the oppositions carefully and then gave them room to breathe.

USA // The New Design Project

Los Feliz Residence

The interior of this residence in Los Feliz, a refuge of the creative class in Los Angeles, is defined by expressive and bespoke contemporary materials or hand-picked vintage objects, furnishings, and artwork. DISC Interiors, for example, dressed the walls of the powder room with custom drapery paired with a hyper-graphic wallpaper made by British wallcoverings workshop Cole & Son. In the master bath, the designers fashioned vanities from a combination of white oak, brass, and Carrara marble and tiled the floor with hexagonal Carrara tiles. Many objects in the guest room were discovered in local vintage stores like the chair by Swedish designer Bruno Mathsson. The bench was already part of the owners' personal collection and the terrarium was also found locally. The purpose-made drapery is burlap linen that was paired with a Moroccan rug and vintage etchings. In the living room, the designers brought together a custom sectional in gray pinstriped velvet with storied objects, original artwork and, not least, flooring made from wall-to-wall seagrass. This cherry-picking of materials and furniture, the inclusion of the client's own belongings, and careful attention to the creation of special new custom items makes the house both contemporary and unique, a translation of personality into space.

USA // DISC Interiors

"It cannot be commercial," designer Kiko Salomão's two young clients told him before his renovation of their São Paulo apartment.

Visitors are greeted by a one-ton stainless steel screen facing the door, the form of which is echoed in the bedroom, with a relief pattern on the wall and again, in smaller scale, on the artwork hung above the living room sofa. Whereas much of the upholstery and surfaces are neutral and muted, receding, or transparent, the rooms are punctuated with objects and artwork that bring them to life: a faceted blue globe light, ceramics with jewel-tone glazes, canvases made from lenticular color fields. Working with irregular footprints in all rooms, Salamao's team was also tasked with creating a "gourmet" kitchen and another secondary, but fully functional, kitchen and used a burnt orange reminiscent of the 1950s. For a Brazilian, the interiors of Project 910, as the apartment came to be called, are minimalist, but they feel alive with forms, textures, and a subdued palette shot through with color.

Brazil // Kiko Salomão

Amsterdam Loft

A cross between a Damien Hirst artwork and a cabinet of curiosities— except someone lives in it.

This private residence designed by Uxus in a 250 sqm, mid-18th-century sugar warehouse sits along an Amsterdam canal with a rare panoramic view over the city. The 250-year-old structure was preserved and respected as much as possible by maintaining the original open-plan organization and by hanging a series of long heavy Italian linen curtains between the beams to created discrete "rooms." At night, the rooms become a phalanx of glowing lanterns.

Uxus used antique beds, an Indonesian wooden cabinet found at a flea market, vintage 1950s lighting, and a 19th-century dinner table with 17th-century garden table legs, along with sculpture and art. The result is an interior with an Old Master chiaroscuro and compositions that juxtapose new and old, thereby enriching both. A sense of discovery draws guests through the space because the function of the objects is not always readily apparent and each contrast becomes engrossing instead of disjunctive, calm instead of cacophonous.

Uxus prides itself on making "emotional and intelligent design" and this project exemplifies it. The curiosity-invoking interior elements were chosen to suit the "eclectic tastes" of the owners, but for Uxus' "eclectic" does not mean loud, pop, shallow, or quirky. Contrasts are not tiled together; instead the designers wove them into a single textile, refined and dominated by the existing wood and curtains, which together become a canvas for each object's authenticity.

Netherlands // Uxus

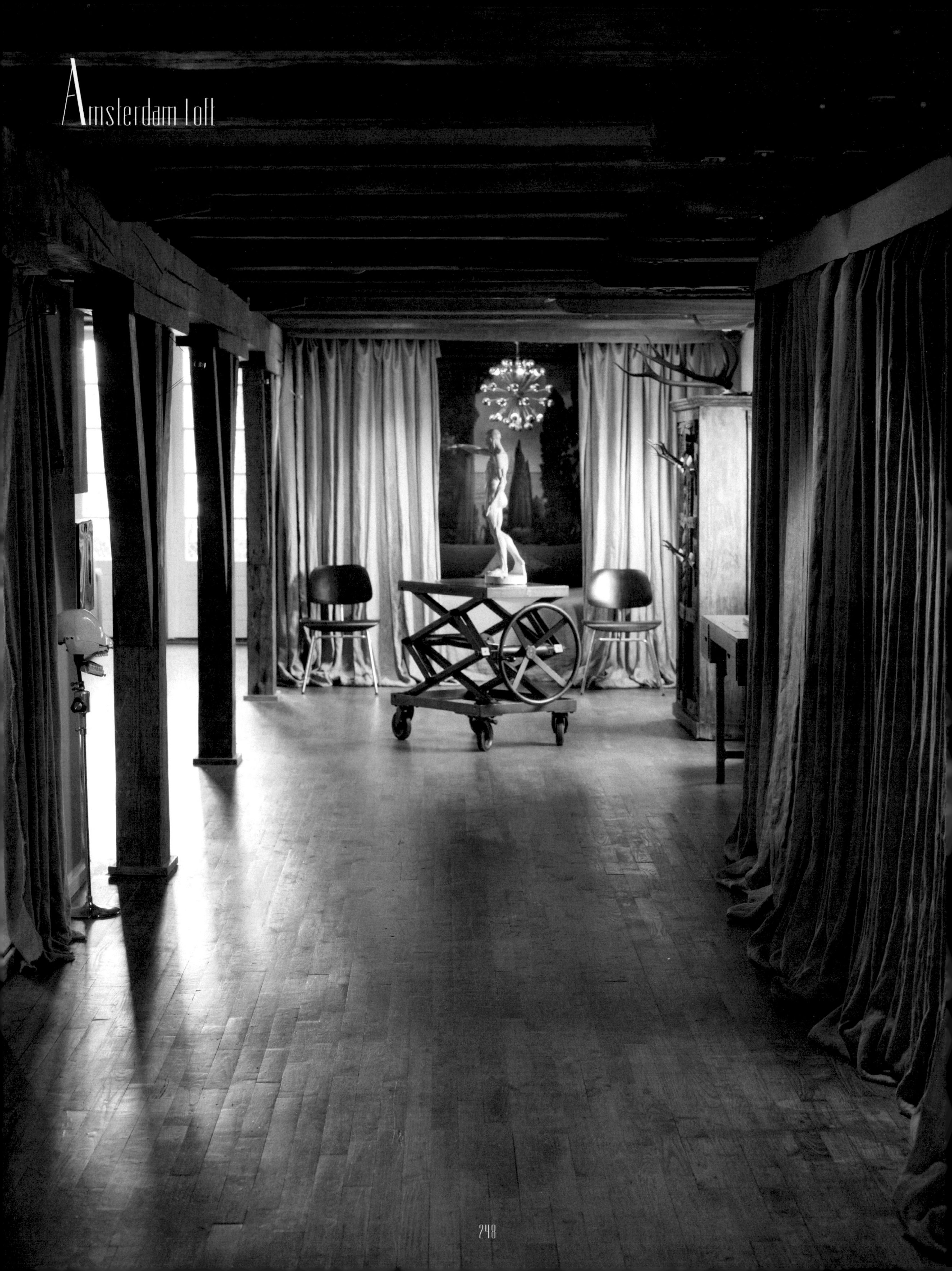

Index

The Chamber of Curiosity

Apartment Design and the New Elegance

This book was conceived, edited, and designed by Gestalten.
Edited by Sven Ehmann, Robert Klanten, and Sofia Borges
Preface and texts by Shonquis Moreno

Layout and design by Nicole Kuderer
Cover by Nicole Kuderer
Cover photography by Cécil Mathieu

Typefaces: High Times by Tilo Pentzin
(Foundry: www.gestaltenfonts.com),
Avenir by Adrian Frutiger

Proofreading by English Express

Printed by Eberl, Immenstadt/Allgäu
Made in Germany

Published by Gestalten, Berlin 2014
ISBN 978-3-89955-517-2

© Die Gestalten Verlag GmbH & Co. KG, Berlin 2014

Bibliographic information published by the Deutsche
Nationalbibliothek.
The Deutsche Nationalbibliothek lists this publication
in the Deutsche Nationalbibliografie;
detailed bibliographic data are available online
at http://dnb.d-nb.de.

This book was printed on paper certified by the FSC®.

Gestalten is a climate-neutral company. We collaborate with the
non-profit carbon offset provider myclimate (www.myclimate.org)
to neutralize the company's carbon footprint produced through
our worldwide business activities by investing in projects that
reduce CO_2 emissions
(www.gestalten.com/myclimate).